mini

FOR ORGANS, PIANOS & ELECTRONIC KEYBOARDS

E-Z PLAY® TODAY

1

ISBN 978-1-4950-7718-0

7777 W. BLUEMOUND RD. P.O. BOX 13819 MILWAUKEE, WI 53213

Visit Hal Leonard Online at
www.halleonard.com

CONTENTS

All I Ask of You
from THE PHANTOM OF THE OPERA

Registration 3
Rhythm: Ballad

Music by Andrew Lloyd Webber
Lyrics by Charles Hart
Additional Lyrics by Richard Stilgoe

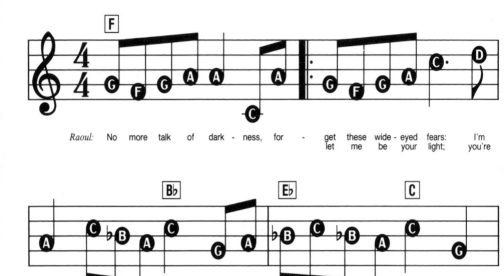

Raoul: No more talk of dark - ness, for - get these wide - eyed fears: I'm
let me be your light; you're

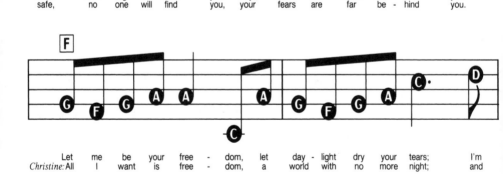

here, noth - ing can harm you, my words will warm and calm you.
safe, no one will find you, your fears are far be - hind you.

Let me be your free - dom, let day - light dry your tears; I'm
Christine: All I want is free - dom, a world with no more night; and

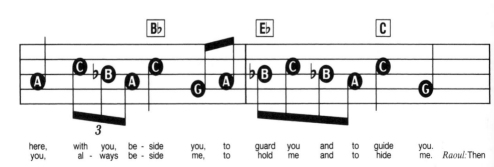

here, with you, be - side you, to guard you and to guide you.
you, al - ways be - side me, to hold me and to hide me. Raoul: Then

5

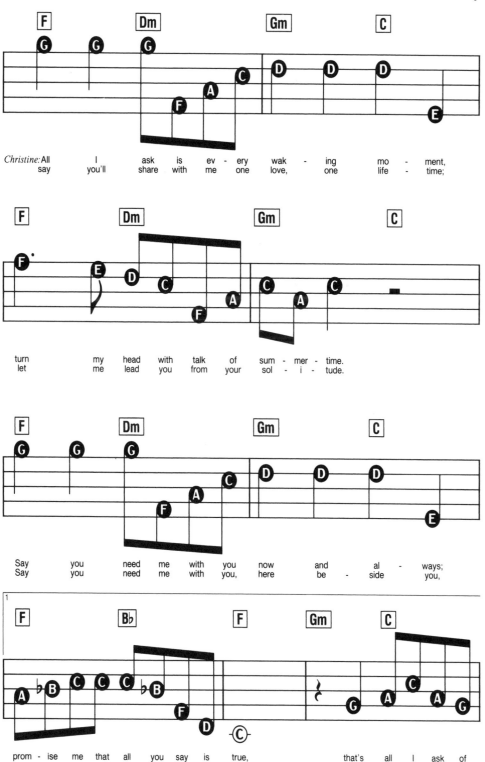

Christine: All I ask is ev - ery wak - ing mo - ment,
say you'll share with me one love, one life - time;

turn my head with talk of sum - mer - time.
let me lead you from your sol - i - tude.

Say you need me with you now and al - ways;
Say you need me with you, here be - side you,

prom - ise me that all you say is true, that's all I ask of

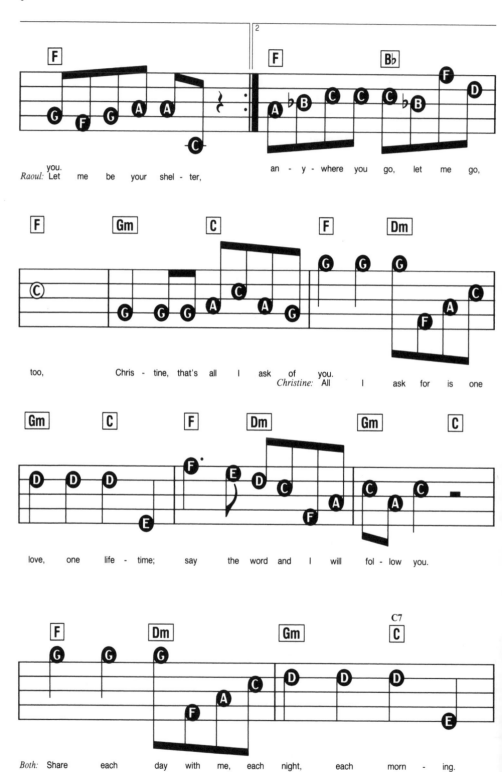

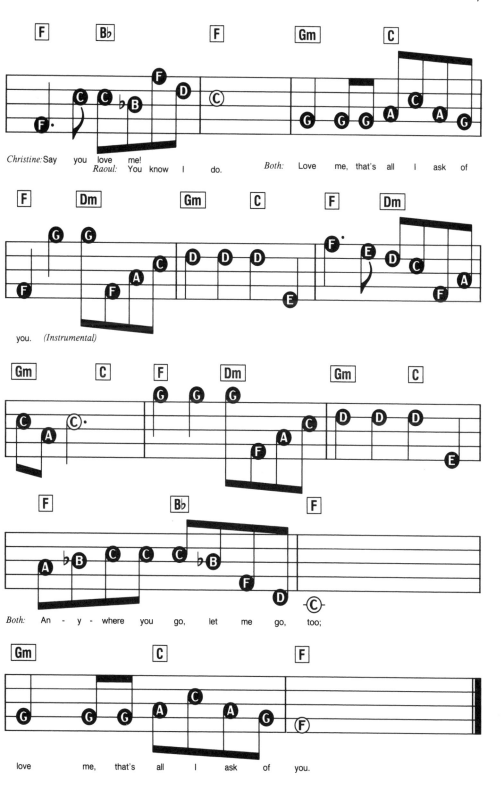

All the Things You Are
from VERY WARM FOR MAY

Registration 2
Rhythm: Ballad or Swing

Lyrics by Oscar Hammerstein II
Music by Jerome Kern

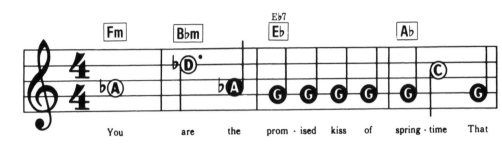

You are the prom - ised kiss of spring - time That

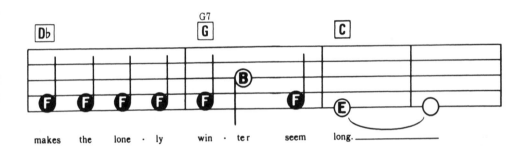

makes the lone - ly win - te r seem long. _____

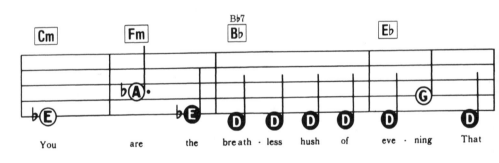

You are the breath - less hush of eve - ning That

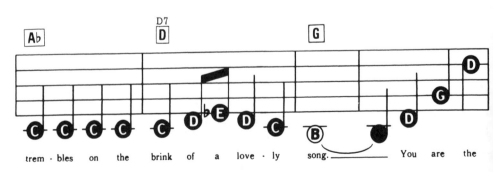

trem - bles on the brink of a love - ly song. _____ You are the

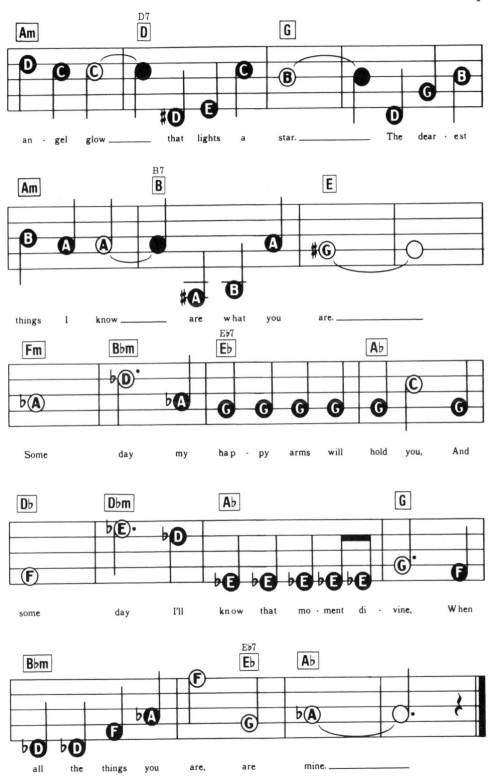

Almost Like Being in Love
from BRIGADOON

Registration 9
Rhythm: Swing

Lyrics by Alan Jay Lerner
Music by Frederick Loewe

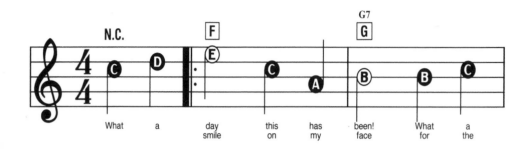

What a day this has been! What a
smile on my face for the

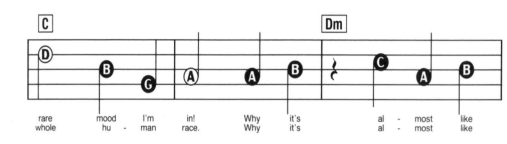

rare mood I'm in! Why it's al - most like
whole hu - man race. Why it's al - most like

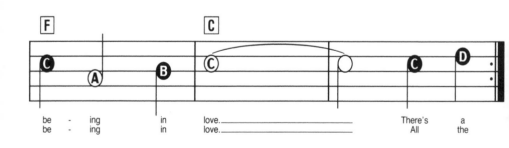

be - ing in love. There's a
be - ing in love. All the

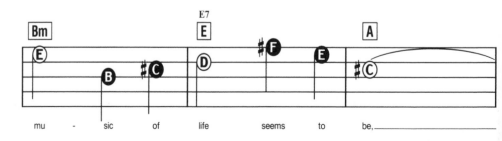

mu - sic of life seems to be,

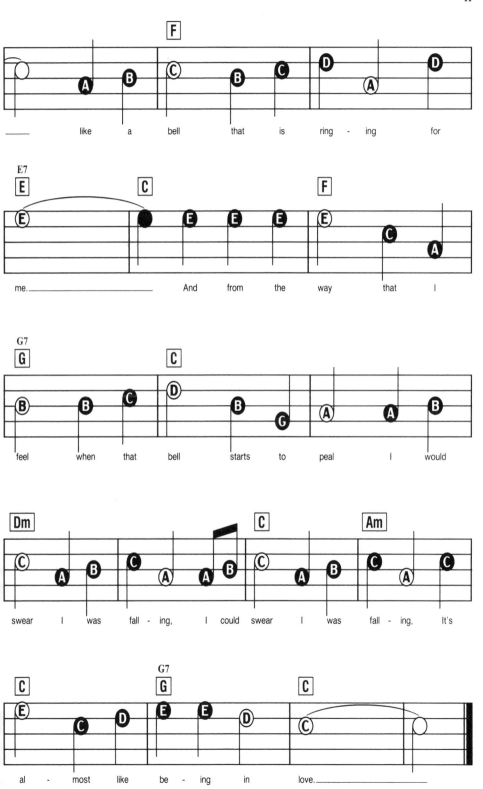

Always

Registration 2
Rhythm: Waltz

Words and Music by
Irving Berlin

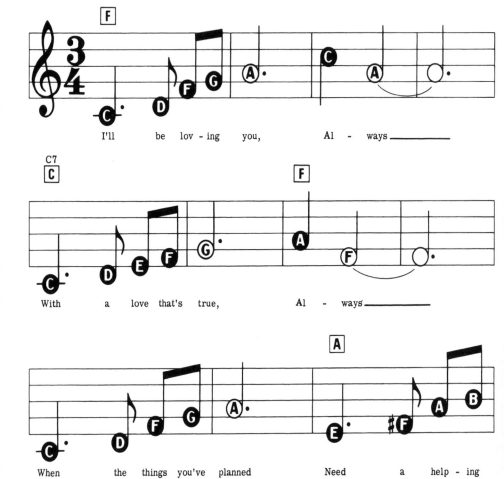

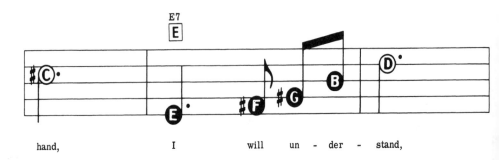

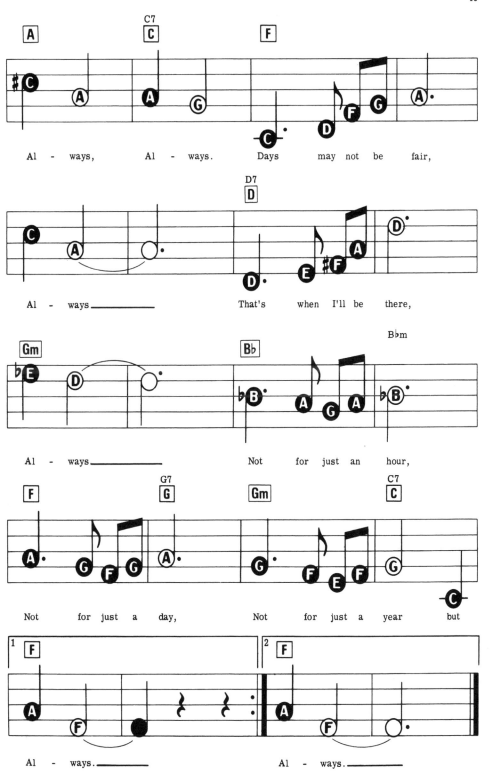

At Last
from ORCHESTRA WIVES

Registration 3
Rhythm: Ballad or Swing

Lyric by Mack Gordon
Music by Harry Warren

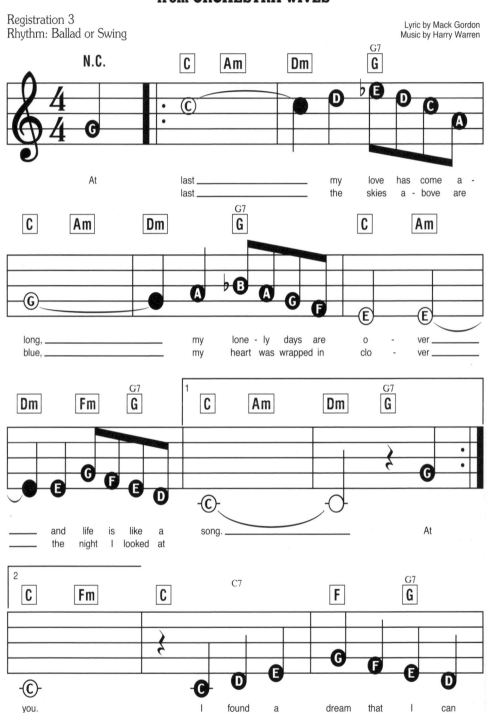

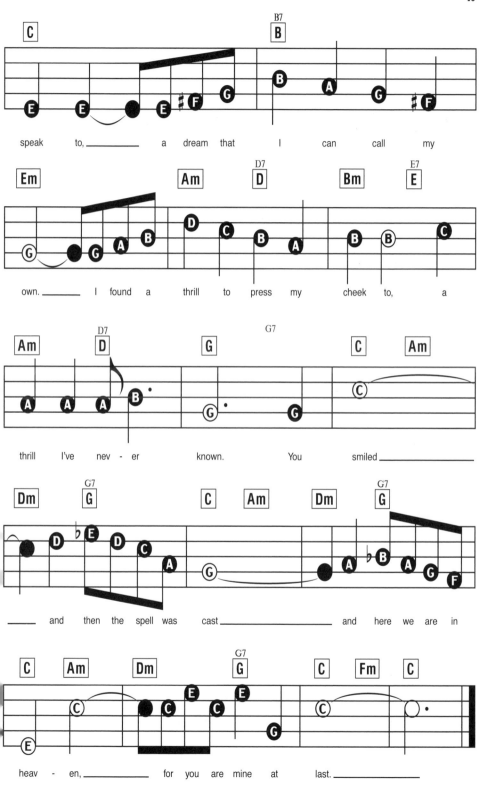

Bewitched
from PAL JOEY

Registration 10
Rhythm: Ballad or Fox Trot

Words by Lorenz Hart
Music by Richard Rodgers

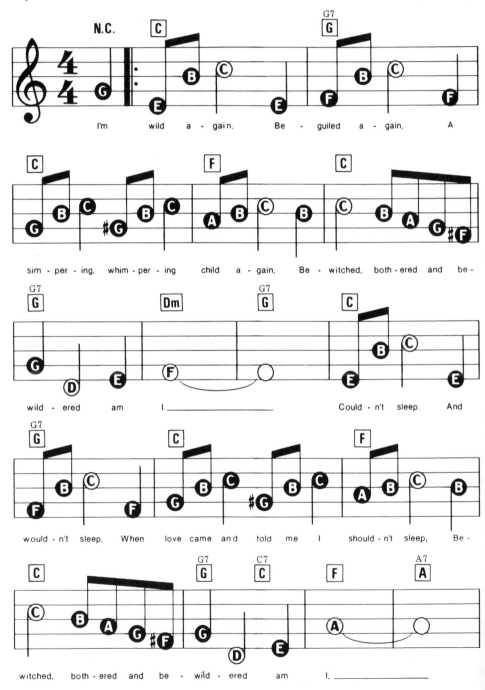

17

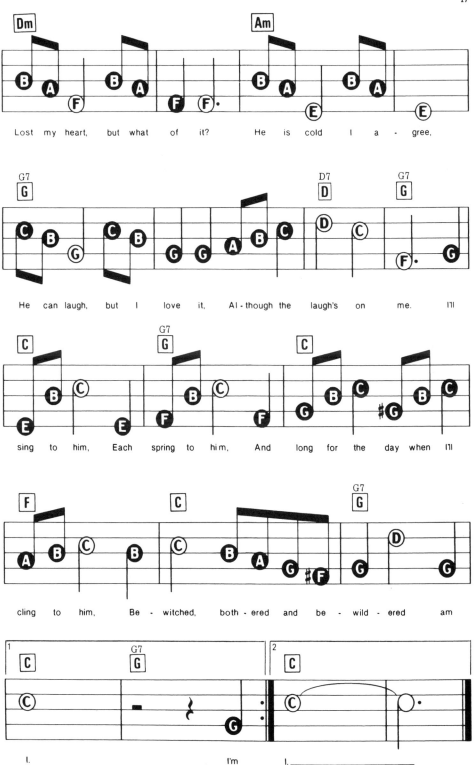

Blue Skies
from BETSY

Registration 8
Rhythm: Fox Trot or Swing

Words and Music by
Irving Berlin

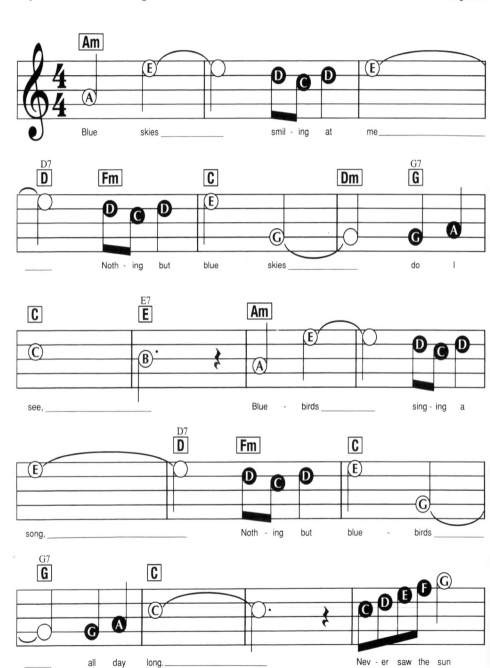

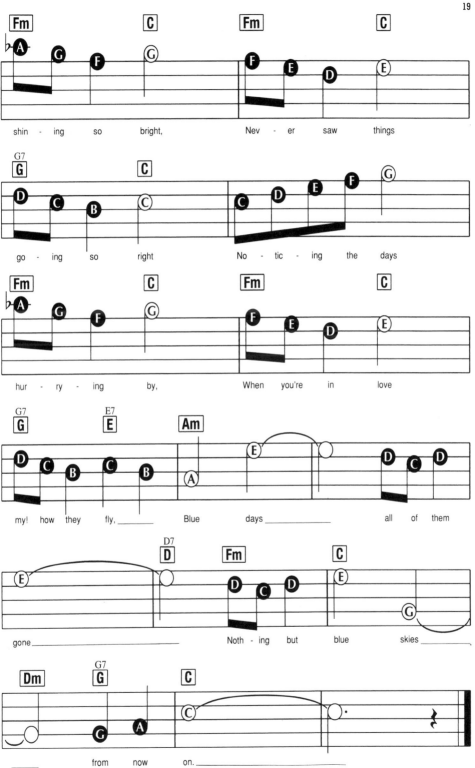

Body and Soul

Registration 8
Rhythm: Ballad

Words by Edward Heyman,
Robert Sour and Frank Eyton
Music by John Green

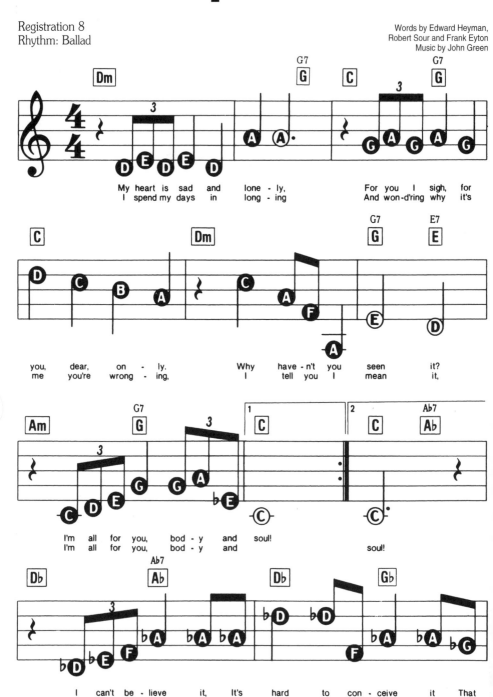

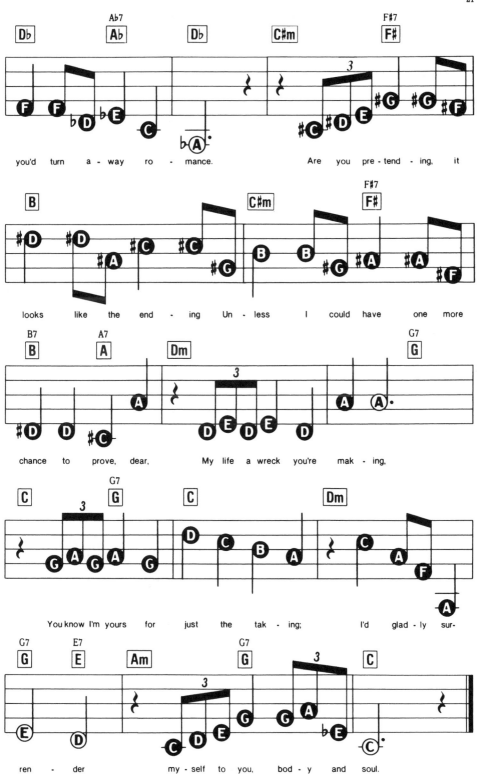

Call Me Irresponsible
from the Paramount Picture PAPA'S DELICATE CONDITION

Registration 8
Rhythm: Swing or Ballad

Words by Sammy Cahn
Music by James Van Heusen

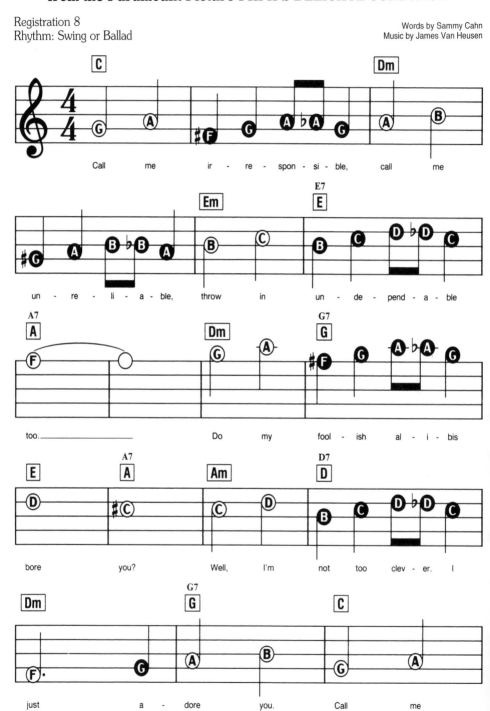

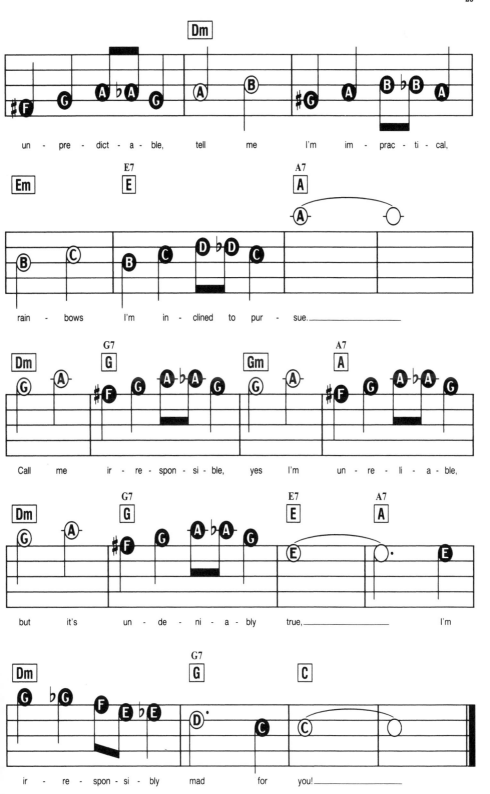

Can't Help Falling in Love

from the Paramount Picture BLUE HAWAII

Registration 3
Rhythm: Ballad or Swing

Words and Music by George David Weiss,
Hugo Peretti and Luigi Creatore

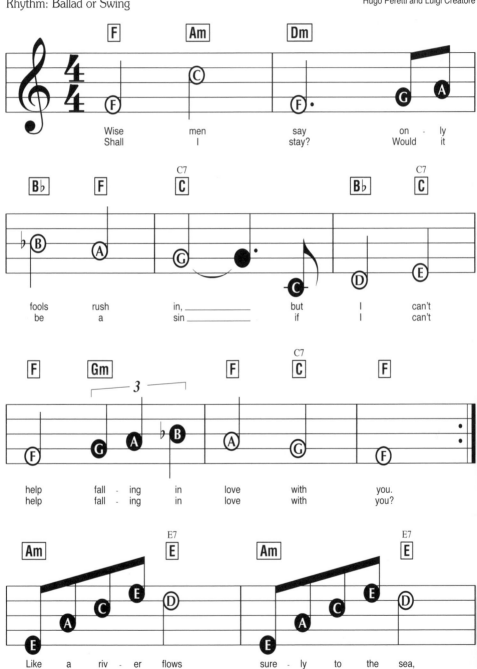

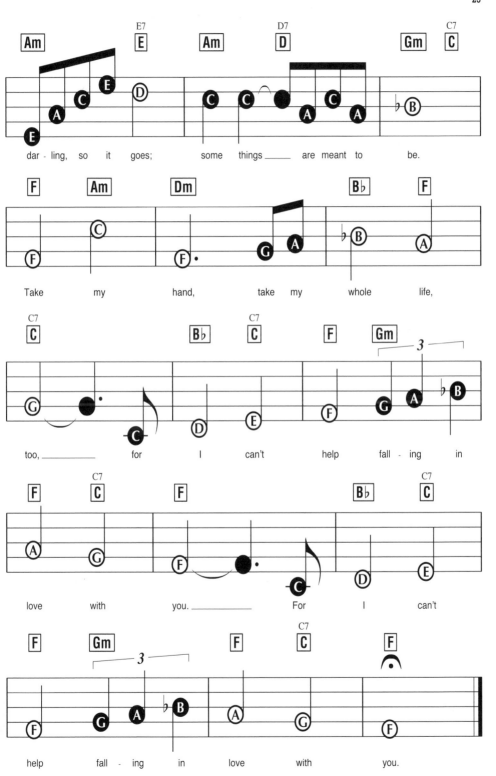

Candle in the Wind

Registration 8
Rhythm: Ballad

Words and Music by Elton John
and Bernie Taupin

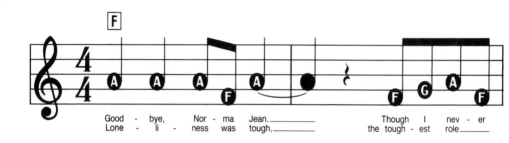

Good - bye, Nor - ma Jean. Though I nev - er
Lone - li - ness was tough, the tough - est role

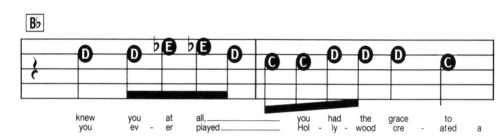

knew you at all, you had the grace to
you ev - er played Hol - ly - wood cre - at ed a

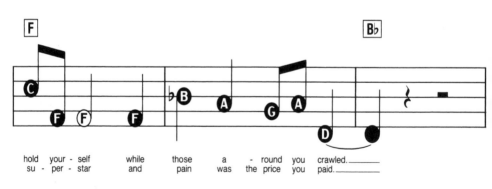

hold your - self while those a - round you crawled.
su - per - star and pain was the price you paid.

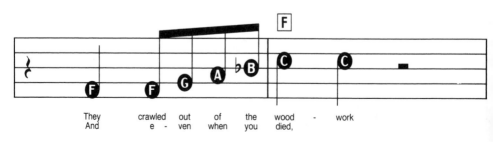

They crawled out of the wood - work
And e - ven when you died,

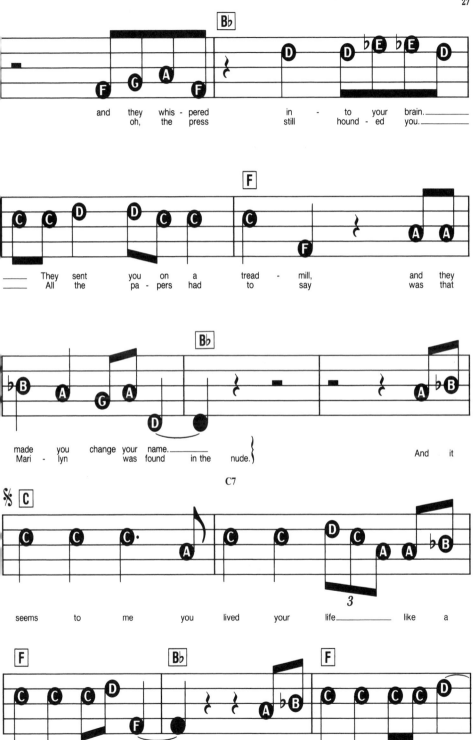

28

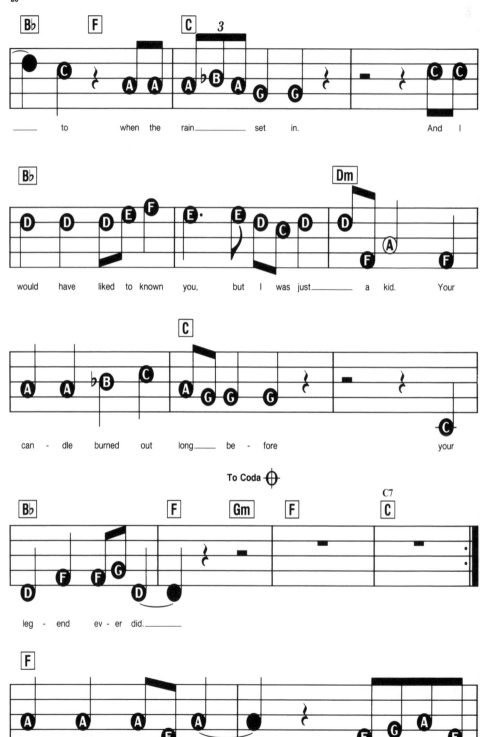

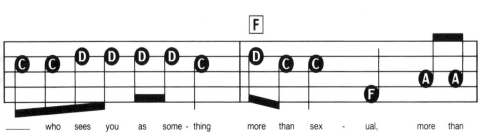

D.S. al Coda
(Return to §
Play to ⊕ and
skip to Coda)

just   our   Mar - i - lyn   Mon - roe.   And   it

CODA

I   would   have   liked   to   known

you.   Oh, _____   but   I   was   just   a   kid,   Your

can - dle   burned   out   long_____   be - fore_____

your   leg - end   ev - er   did. _____

Imagine

Registration 8
Rhythm: 8-Beat or Rock

Words and Music by
John Lennon

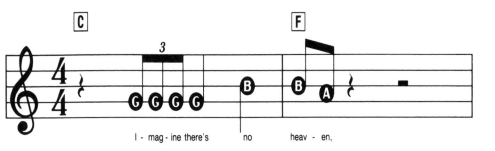

I - mag - ine there's   no   heav - en,

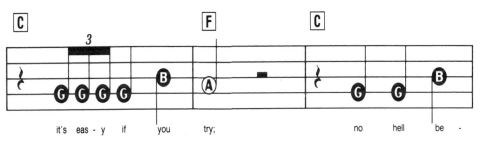

it's eas - y if   you   try;   no   hell   be -

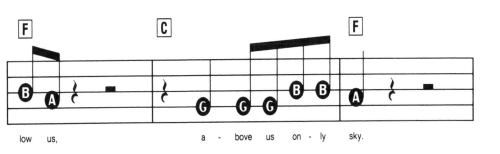

low   us,   a - bove us on - ly   sky.

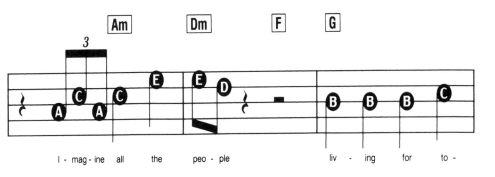

I - mag - ine all   the   peo - ple   liv - ing   for   to -

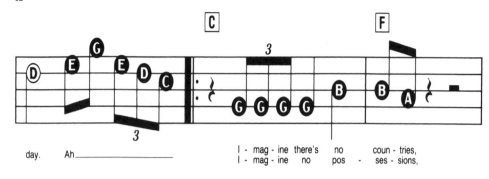

day. Ah_____

I - mag - ine there's no coun - tries,
I - mag - ine no pos - ses - sions,

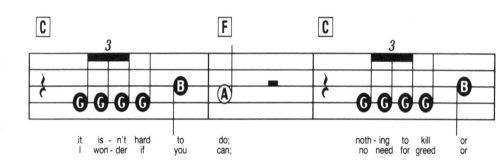

it   is - n't   hard   to   do;   noth - ing   to   kill   or
I   won - der   if   you   can;   no   need   for   greed   or

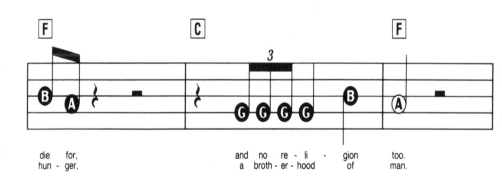

die   for,   and   no   re - li - gion   too.
hun - ger,   a   broth - er - hood   of   man.

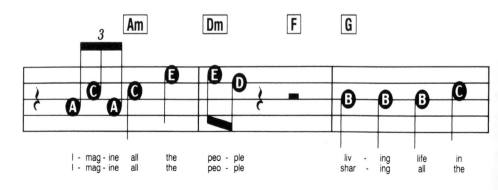

I - mag - ine   all   the   peo - ple   liv - ing   life   in
I - mag - ine   all   the   peo - ple   shar - ing   all   the

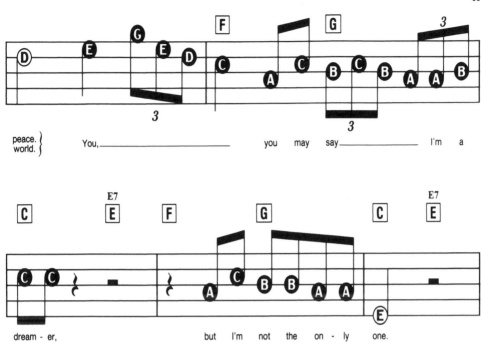

peace.
world.
You,_____ you may say_____ I'm a

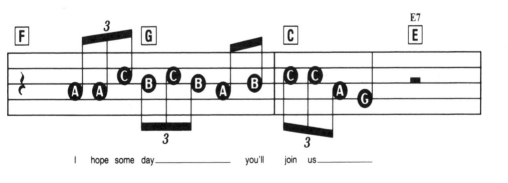

dream - er, but I'm not the on - ly one.

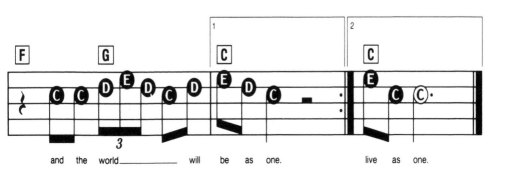

I hope some day_____ you'll join us_____

and the world_____ will be as one. live as one.

Climb Ev'ry Mountain
from THE SOUND OF MUSIC

Registration 5
Rhythm: Swing or Fox Trot

Lyrics by Oscar Hammerstein II
Music by Richard Rodgers

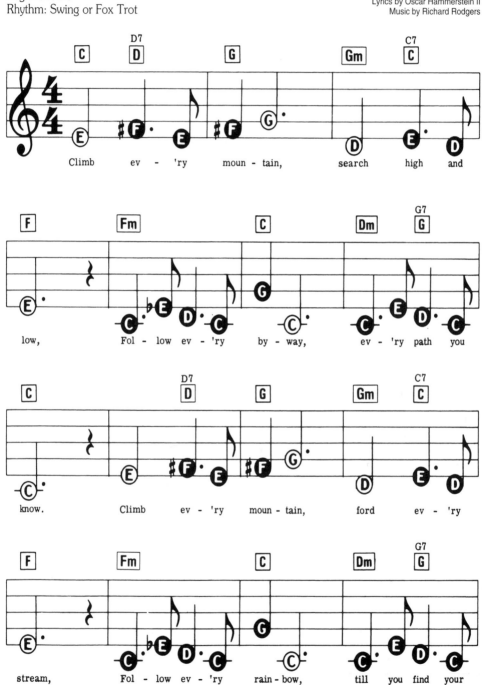

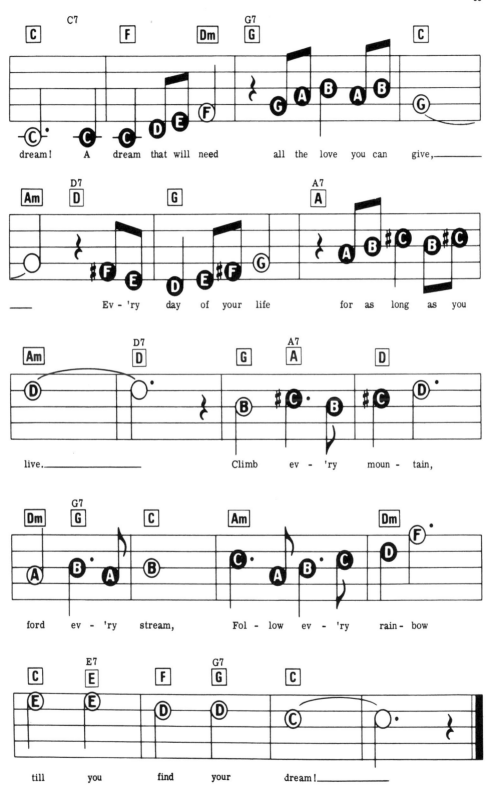

Crazy

Registration 2
Rhythm: Fox Trot or Swing

Words and Music by
Willie Nelson

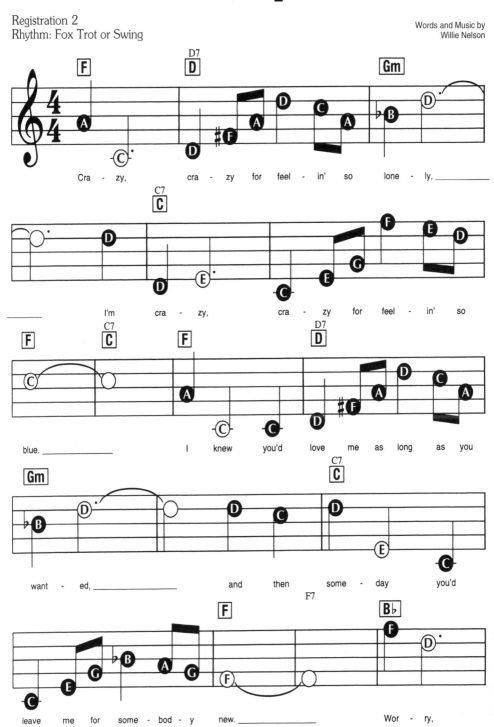

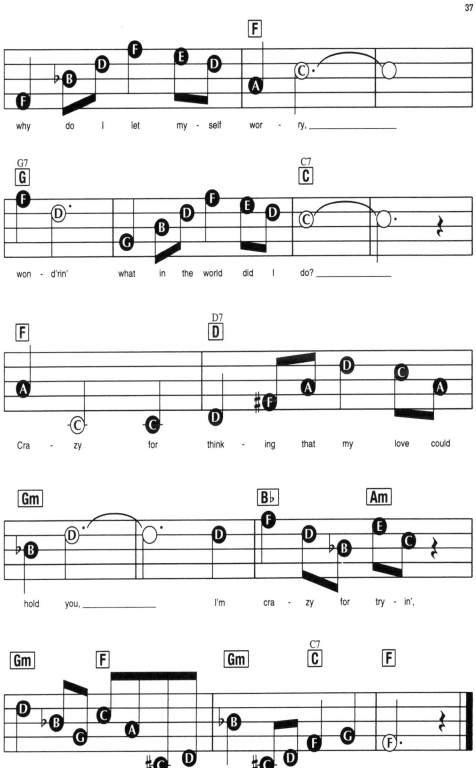

Edelweiss
from THE SOUND OF MUSIC

Registration 4
Rhythm: Waltz

Lyrics by Oscar Hammerstein II
Music by Richard Rodgers

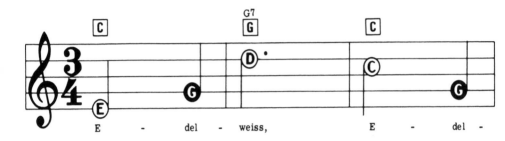

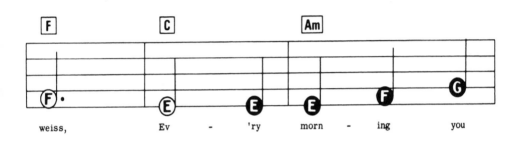

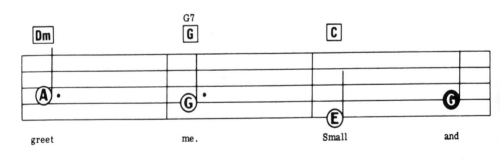

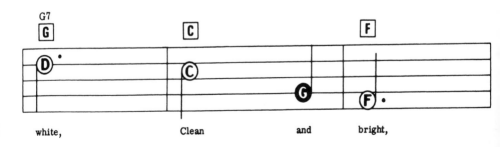

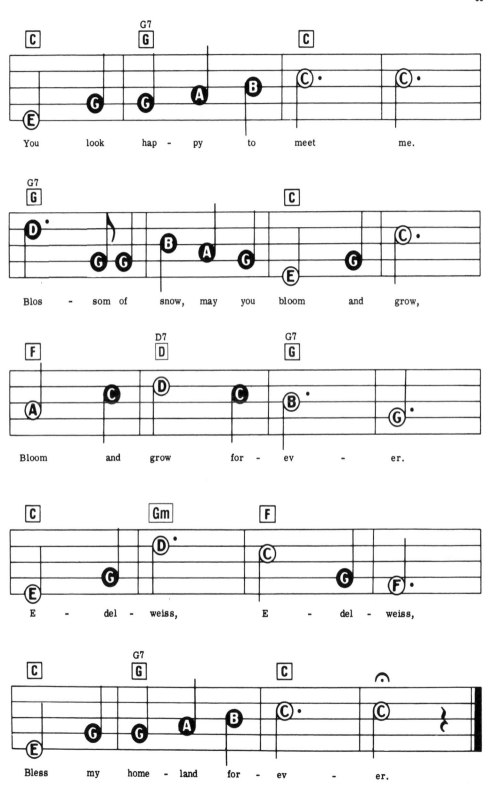

Emily

from the MGM Motion Picture THE AMERICANIZATION OF EMILY

Registration 3
Rhythm: Waltz

Music by Johnny Mandel
Words by Johnny Mercer

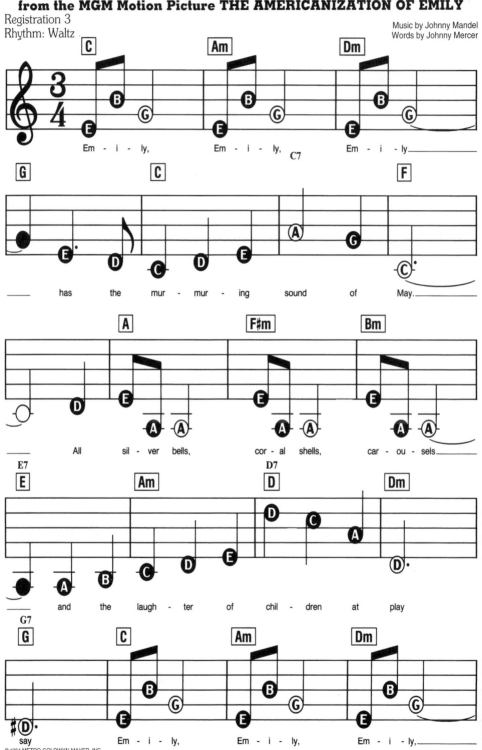

41

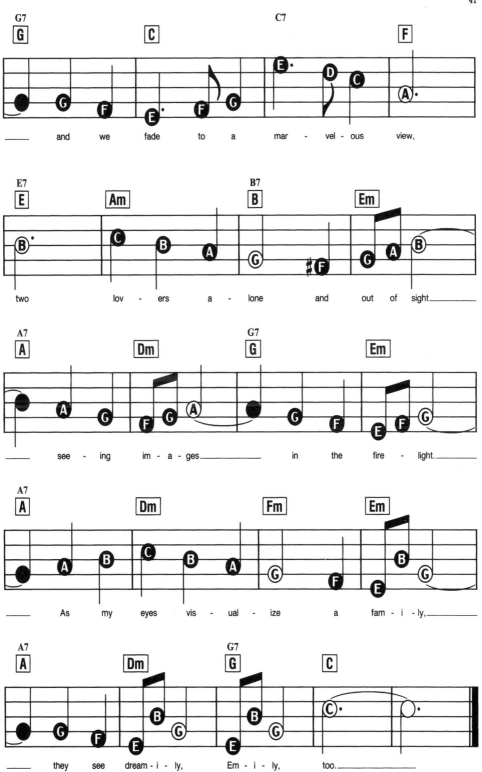

Fly Me to the Moon
(In Other Words)
featured in the Motion Picture ONCE AROUND

Registration 2
Rhythm: Waltz or Jazz Waltz

Words and Music by
Bart Howard

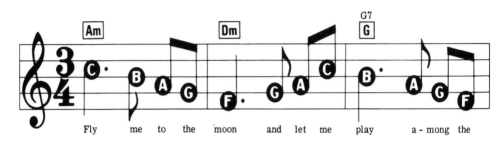

Fly me to the moon and let me play a - mong the

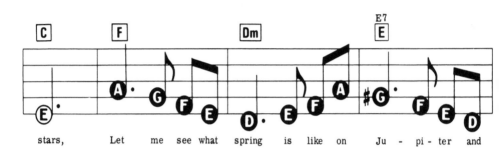

stars, Let me see what spring is like on Ju - pi - ter and

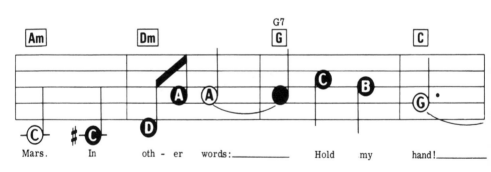

Mars. In oth - er words:_____ Hold my hand!_____

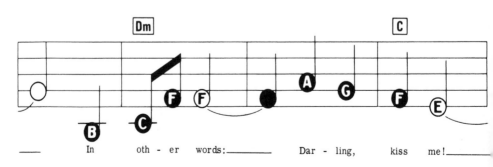

____ In oth - er words:_____ Dar - ling, kiss me!_____

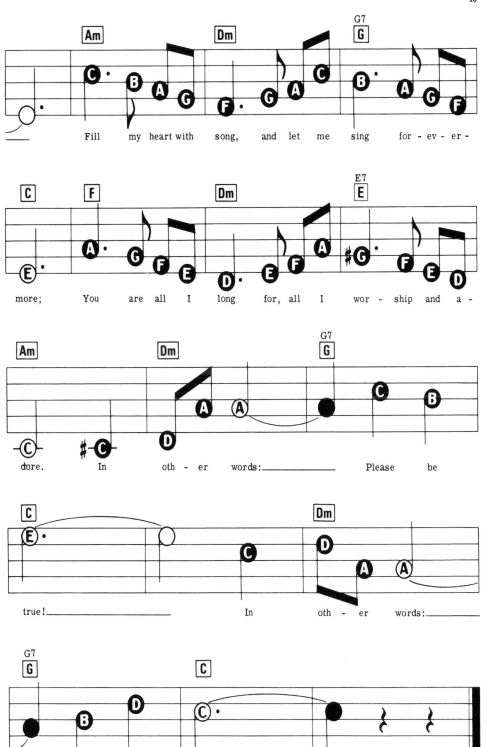

Georgia on My Mind

Registration 4
Rhythm: Swing

Words by Stuart Gorrell
Music by Hoagy Carmichael

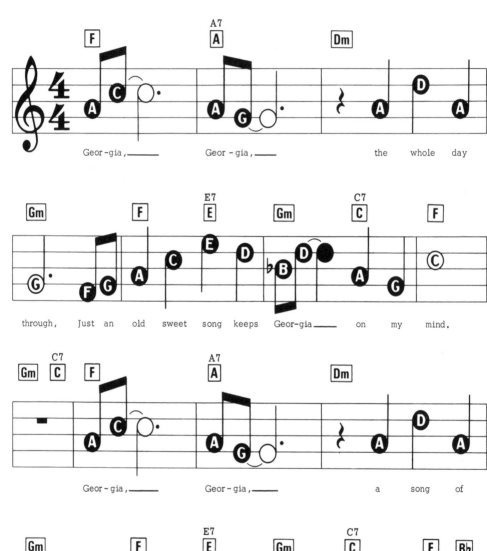

Geor-gia, _____ Geor - gia, _____ the whole day

through, Just an old sweet song keeps Geor-gia_____ on my mind.

Geor - gia, _____ Geor - gia, _____ a song of

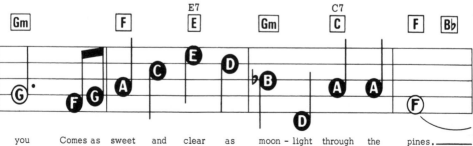

you Comes as sweet and clear as moon - light through the pines. _____

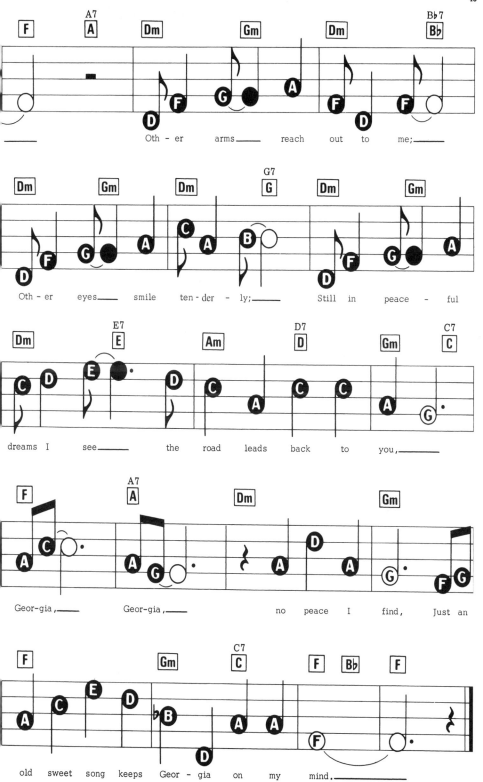

The Girl from Ipanema
(Garôta de Ipanema)

Registration 4
Rhythm: Latin or Bossa Nova

Music by Antonio Carlos Jobim
English Words by Norman Gimbel
Original Words by Vinicius de Moraes

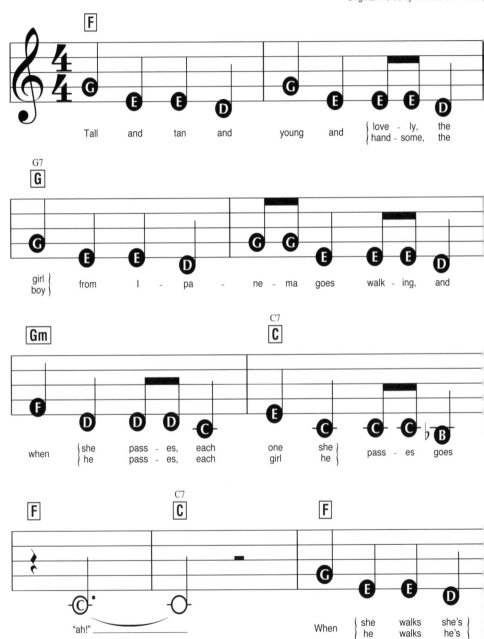

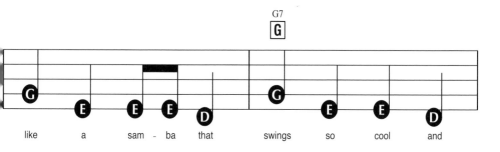

like a sam - ba that swings so cool and

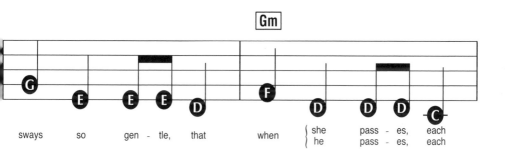

sways so gen - tle, that when { she / he } pass - es, pass - es, each each

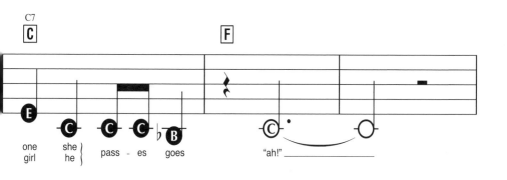

one girl { she / he } pass - es goes "ah!" _____

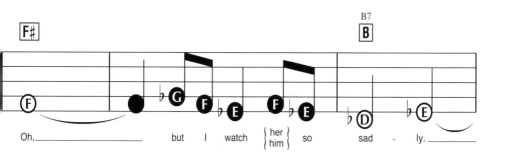

Oh, _____ but I watch { her / him } so sad - ly. _____

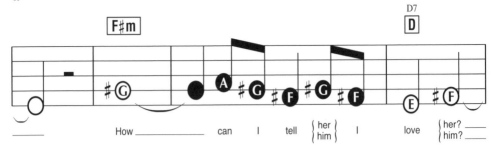

How _____ can I tell { her } { him } I love { her? } _____ { him? } _____

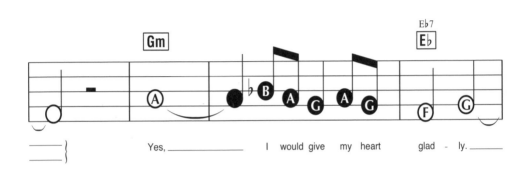

Yes, _____ I would give my heart glad - ly. _____

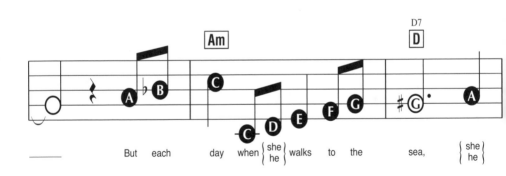

But each day when { she } { he } walks to the sea, { she } { he }

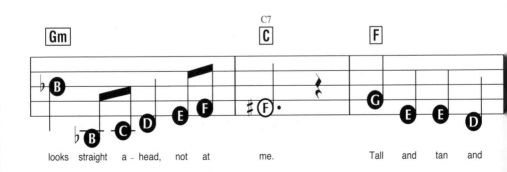

looks straight a - head, not at me. Tall and tan and

49

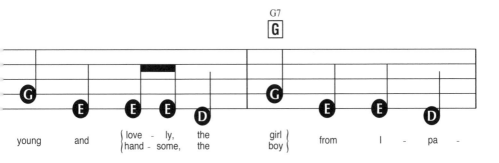

young   and   { love - ly,   the   girl }   from   I   -   pa -
                            { hand - some, the   boy }

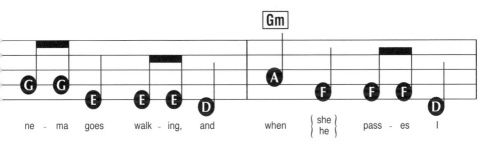

ne - ma   goes   walk - ing,   and   when   { she }   pass - es   I
                                                                { he }

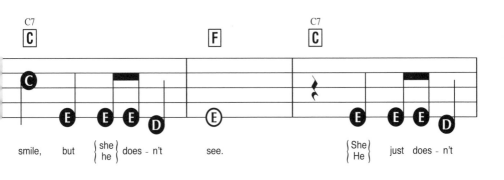

smile,   but   { she }   does - n't   see.   { She }   just does - n't
                     { he }   { He }

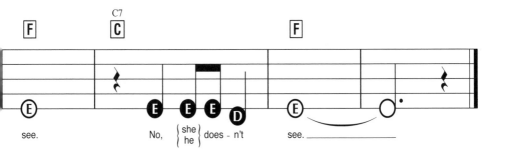

see.   No,   { she }   does - n't   see. _____
                               { he }

Here's That Rainy Day
from CARNIVAL IN FLANDERS

Registration 2
Rhythm: Ballad or Slow Rock

Words by Johnny Burke
Music by Jimmy Van Heusen

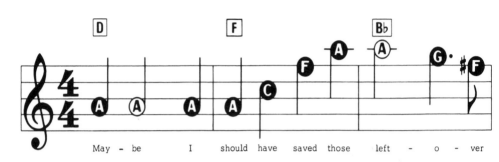

May - be   I   should have   saved those   left - o - ver

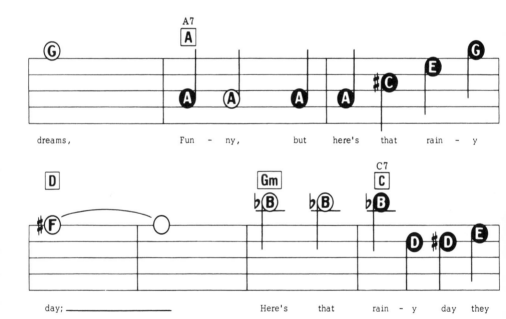

dreams,   Fun - ny,   but   here's   that   rain - y

day; _____   Here's   that   rain - y   day   they

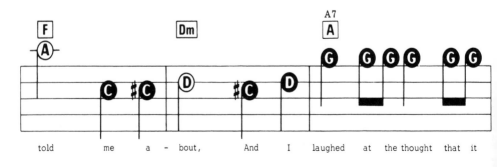

told   me   a - bout,   And   I   laughed   at   the thought   that   it

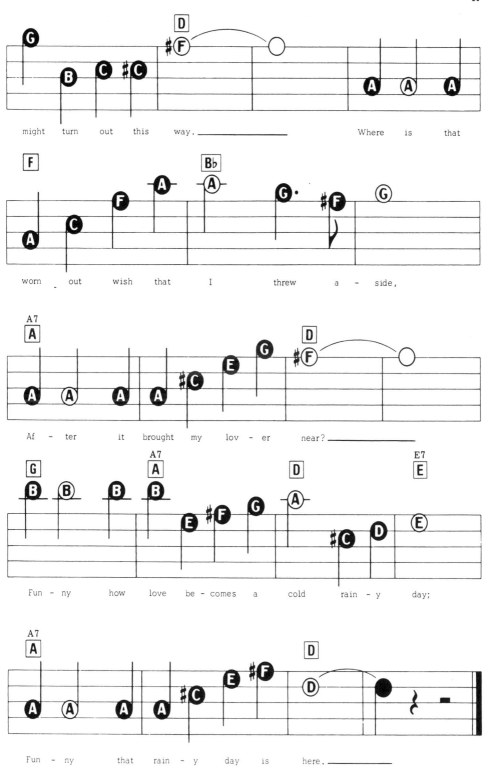

How Deep Is the Ocean
(How High Is the Sky)

Registration 4
Rhythm: Fox Trot or Swing

Words and Music by
Irving Berlin

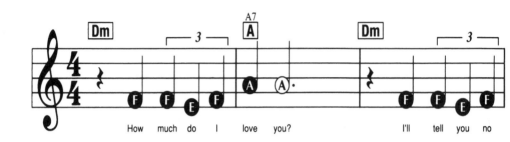

How much do I love you? I'll tell you no

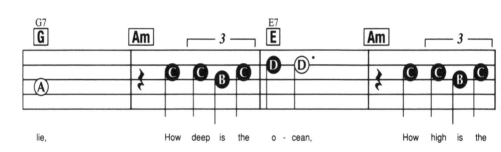

lie, How deep is the o - cean, How high is the

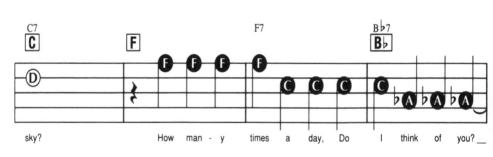

sky? How man - y times a day, Do I think of you? ___

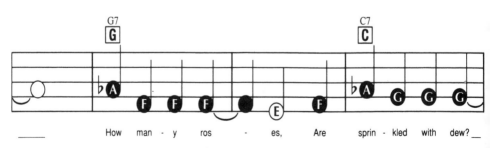

___ How man - y ros - es, Are sprin - kled with dew? ___

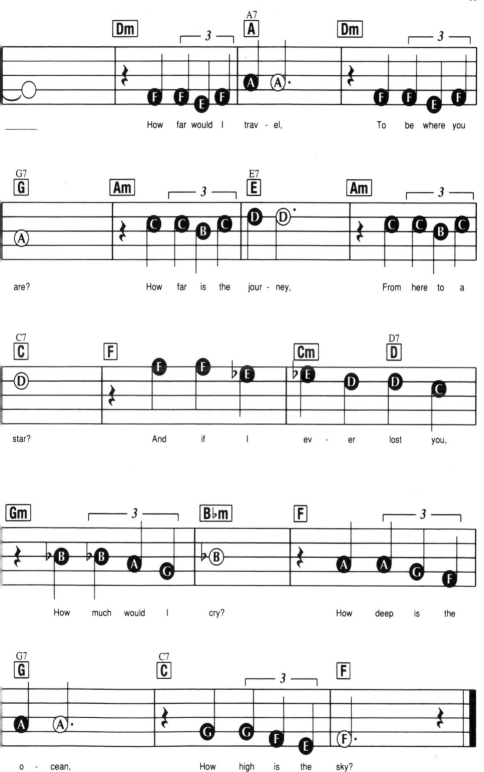

I Dreamed a Dream
from LES MISÉRABLES

Registration 1
Rhythm: Ballad

Music by Claude-Michel Schönberg
Lyrics by Alain Boublil, Jean-Marc Natel and Herbert Kretzmer

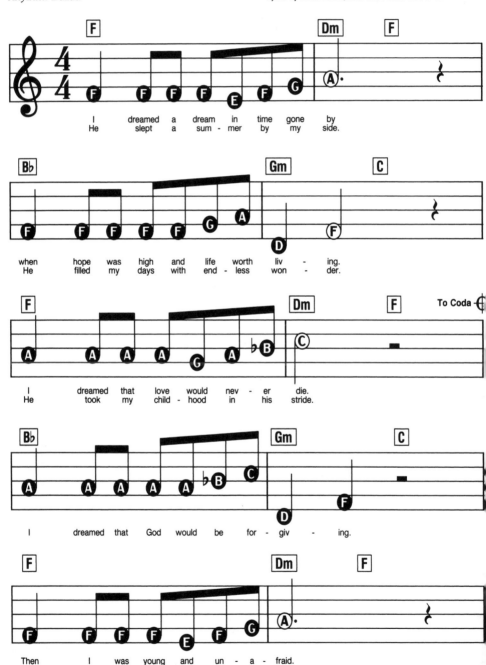

55

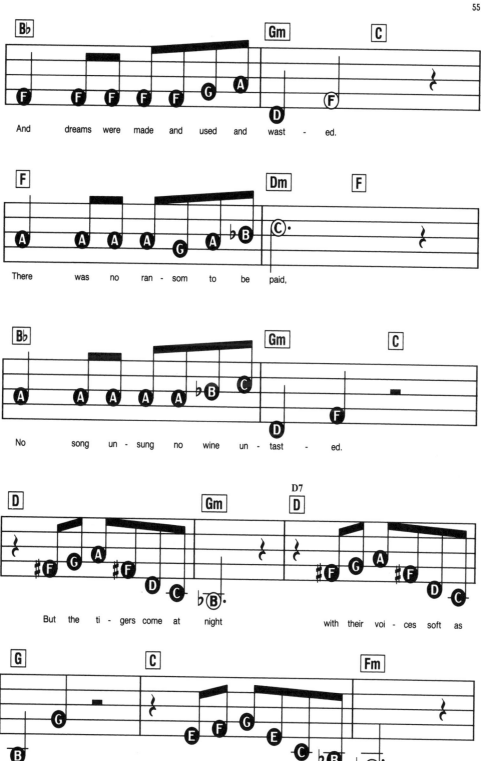

56

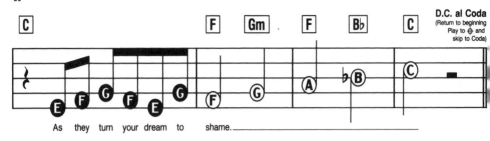

As they turn your dream to shame.

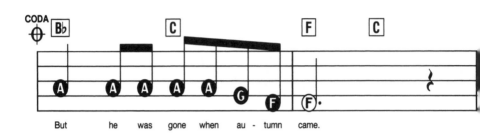

But he was gone when au - tumn came.

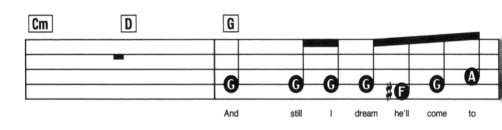

And still I dream he'll come to

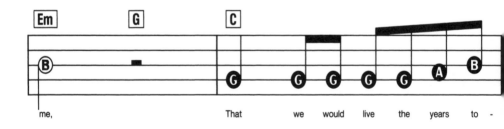

me, That we would live the years to -

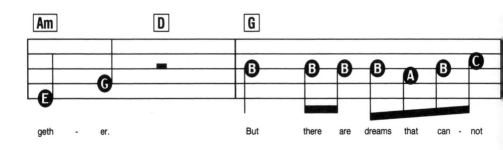

geth - er. But there are dreams that can - not

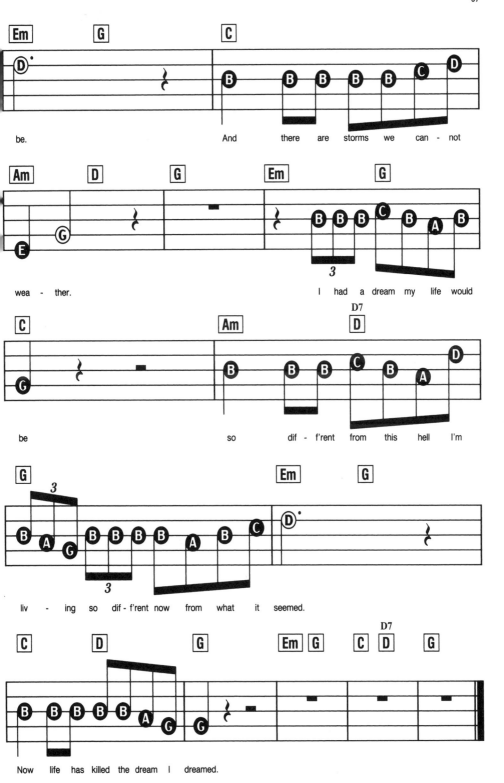

I Left My Heart in San Francisco

Registration 9
Rhythm: Fox Trot

Words by Douglass Cross
Music by George Cory

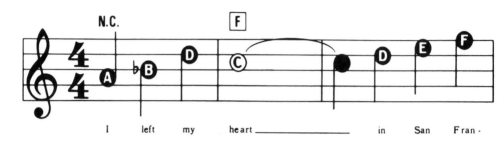

I left my heart _____ in San Fran -

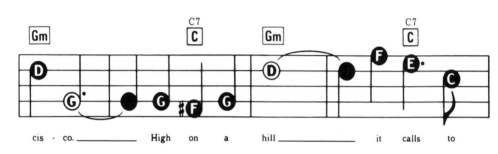

cis - co. _____ High on a hill _____ it calls to

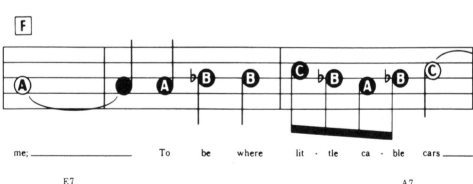

me; _____ To be where lit - tle ca - ble cars _____

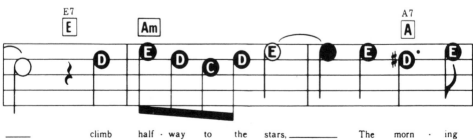

_____ climb half - way to the stars, _____ The morn - ing

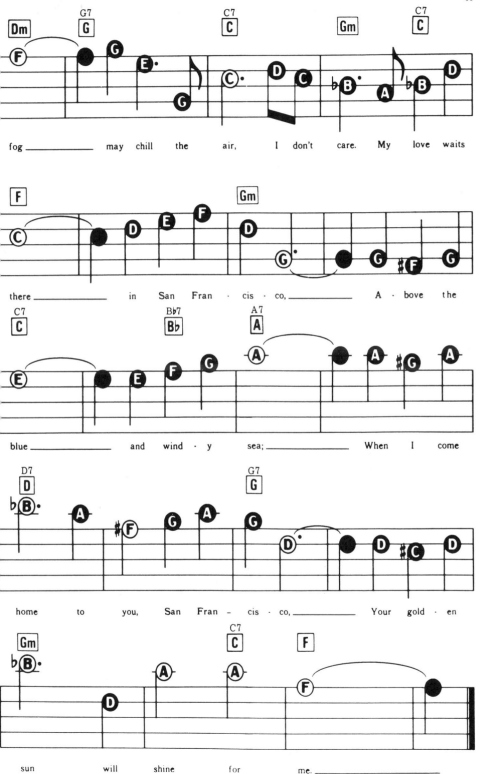

I'll Be Seeing You
from RIGHT THIS WAY

Registration 5
Rhythm: Swing

Written by Irving Kahal
and Sammy Fain

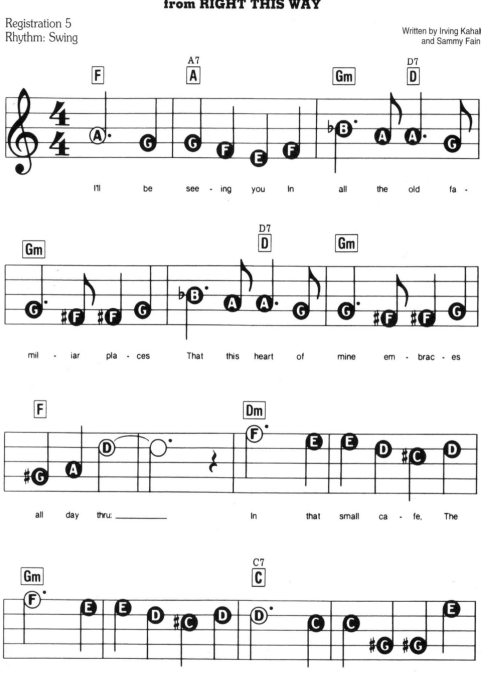

I'll be see - ing you In all the old fa -

mil - iar pla - ces That this heart of mine em - brac - es

all day thru: _____ In that small ca - fe, The

park a - cross the way, The chil - dren's ca - rou - sel, The

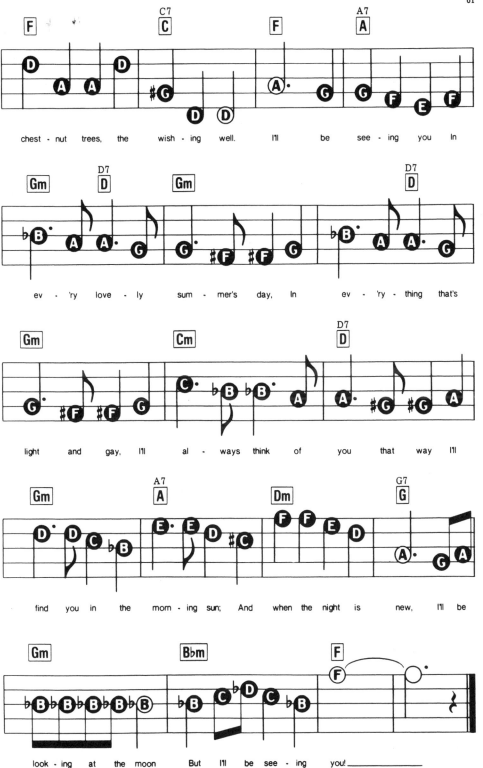

In the Wee Small Hours
of the Morning

Registration 2
Rhythm: Ballad

Words by Bob Hilliard
Music by David Mann

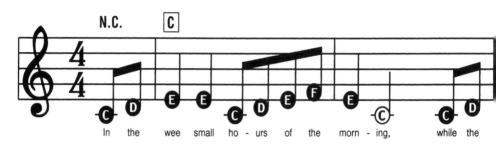

In the wee small ho - urs of the morn - ing, while the

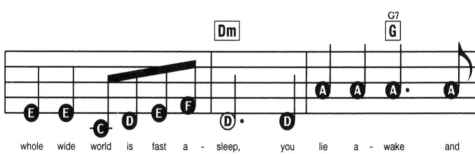

whole wide world is fast a - sleep, you lie a - wake and

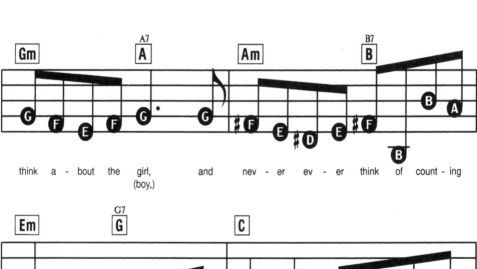

think a - bout the girl, and nev - er ev - er think of count - ing
(boy,)

sheep. When your lone - ly heart has learned its

Isn't It Romantic?

from the Paramount Picture LOVE ME TONIGHT

Registration 2
Rhythm: Swing or Ballad

Words by Lorenz Hart
Music by Richard Rodgers

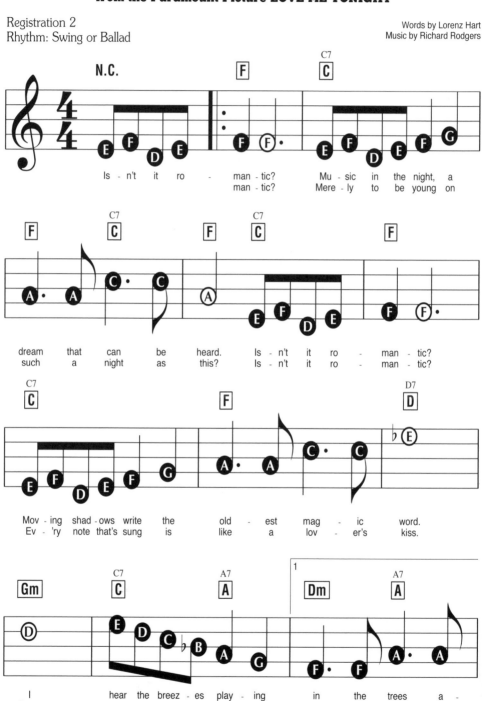

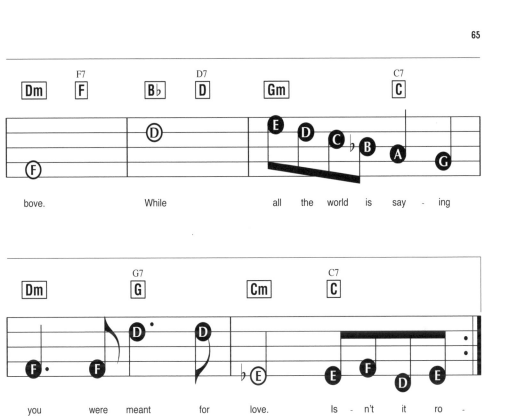

bove.   While   all   the   world   is   say - ing

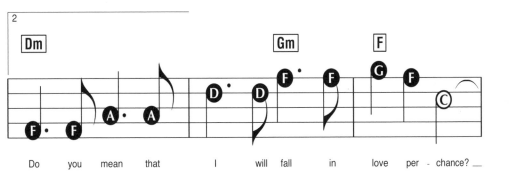

you   were   meant   for   love.   Is - n't   it   ro -

Do   you   mean   that   I   will   fall   in   love   per - chance? __

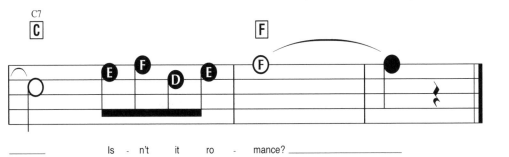

Is - n't   it   ro - mance? _____

It Might as Well Be Spring
from STATE FAIR

Registration 3
Rhythm: Ballad

Lyrics by Oscar Hammerstein II
Music by Richard Rodgers

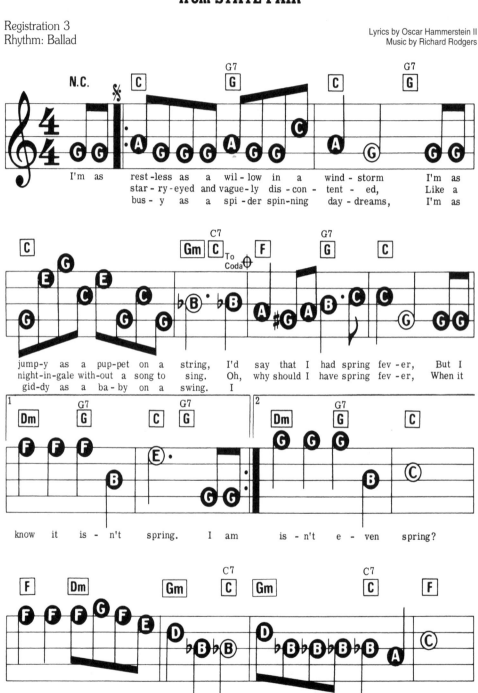

I'm as rest-less as a wil-low in a wind-storm I'm as
star-ry-eyed and vague-ly dis-con-tent-ed, Like a
bus-y as a spi-der spin-ning day-dreams, I'm as

jump-y as a pup-pet on a string, I'd say that I had spring fev-er, But I
night-in-gale with-out a song to sing. Oh, why should I have spring fev-er, When it
gid-dy as a ba-by on a swing. I

know it is-n't spring. I am is-n't e-ven spring?

I keep wish-ing I were some-where else, Walk-ing down a strange, new street,

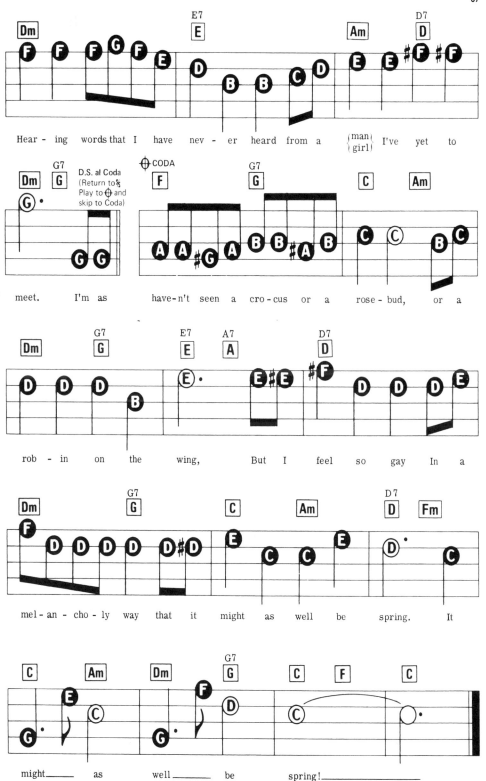

Just the Way You Are

Registration 4
Rhythm: Rock or Jazz Rock

Words and Music by
Billy Joel

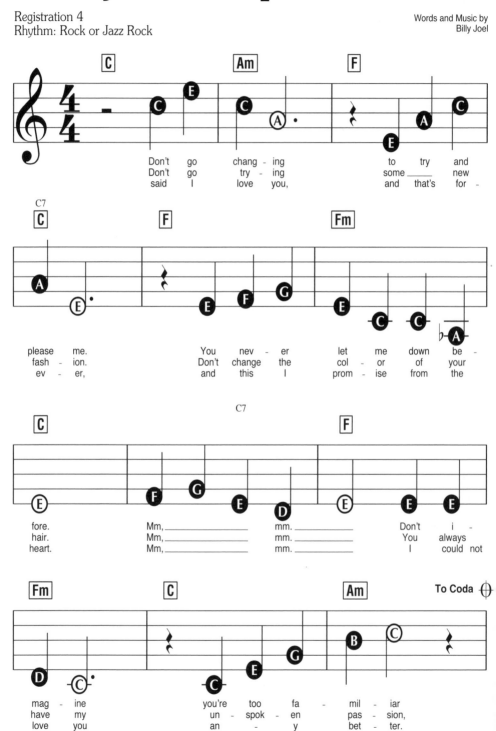

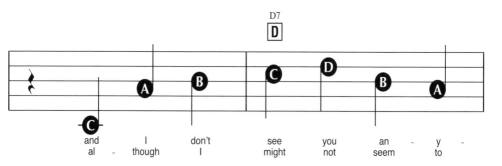

and | don't see you an - y -
al - though I might not seem to

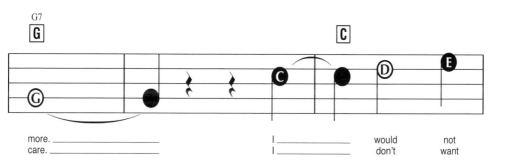

more. I would not
care. I don't want

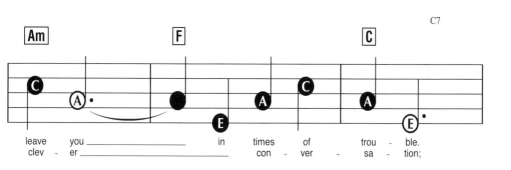

leave you in times of trou - ble.
clev - er con - ver - sa - tion;

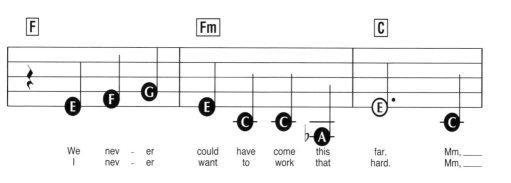

We nev - er could have come this far. Mm, ___
I nev - er want to work that hard. Mm, ___

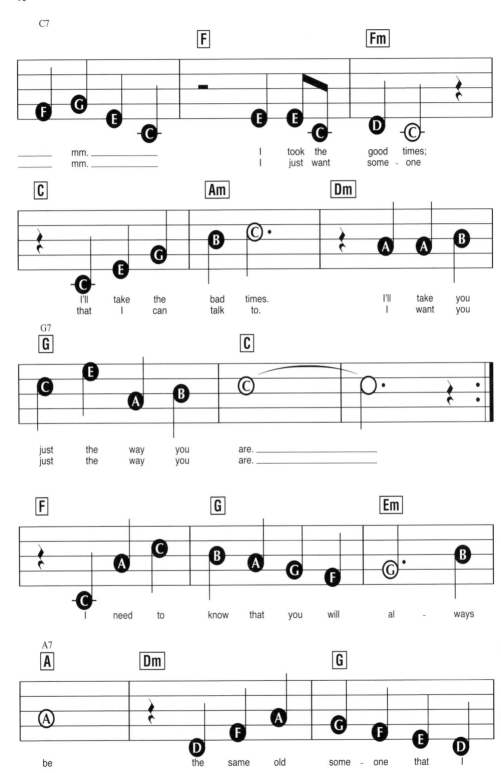

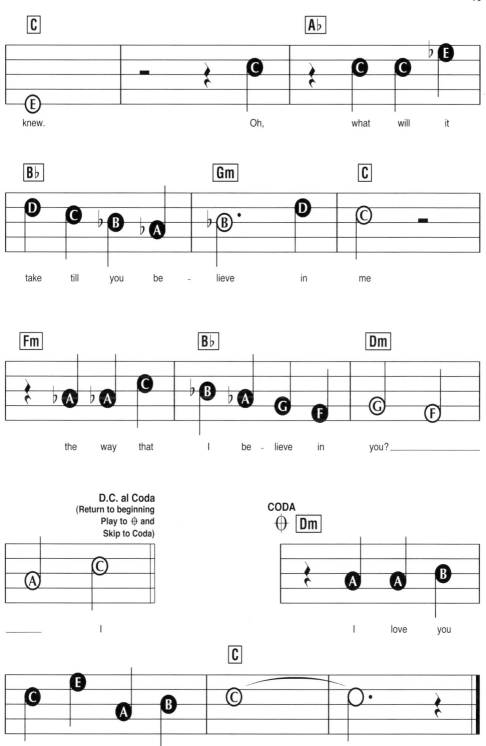

The Lady Is a Tramp
from BABES IN ARMS

Registration 7
Rhythm: Fox Trot or Swing

Words by Lorenz Hart
Music by Richard Rodgers

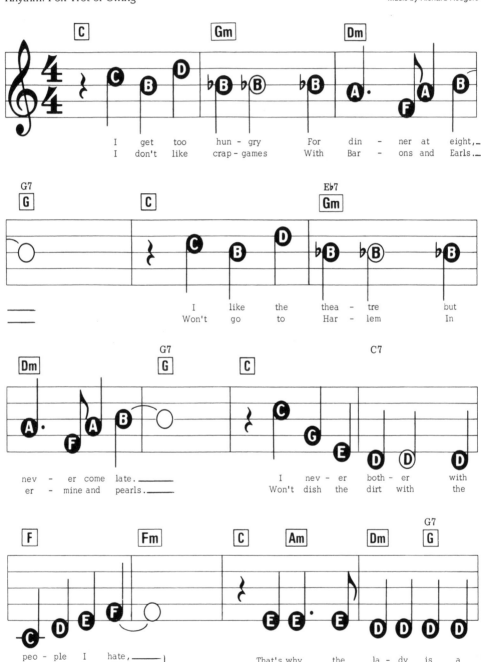

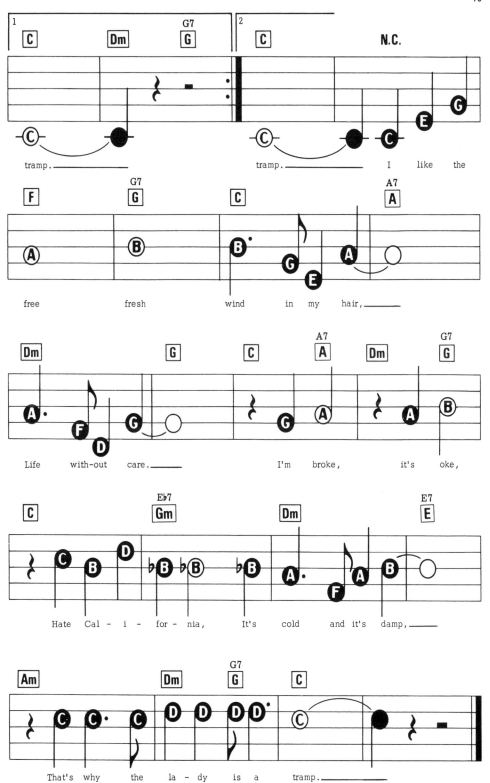

Let It Be

Registration 3
Rhythm: Rock

Words and Music by John Lennon
and Paul McCartney

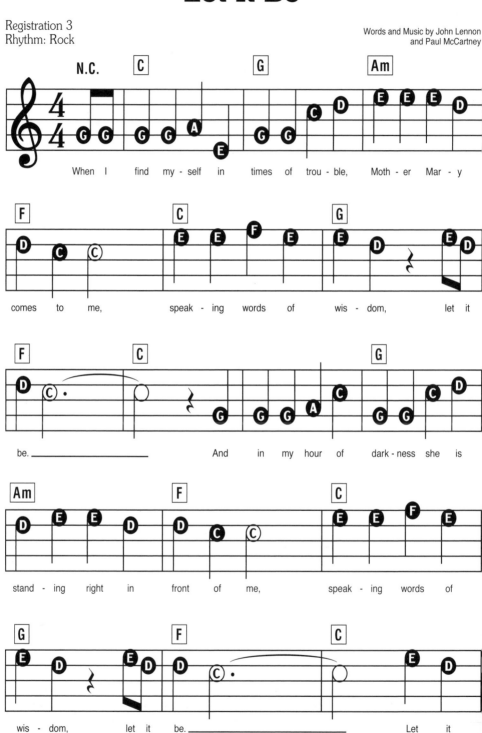

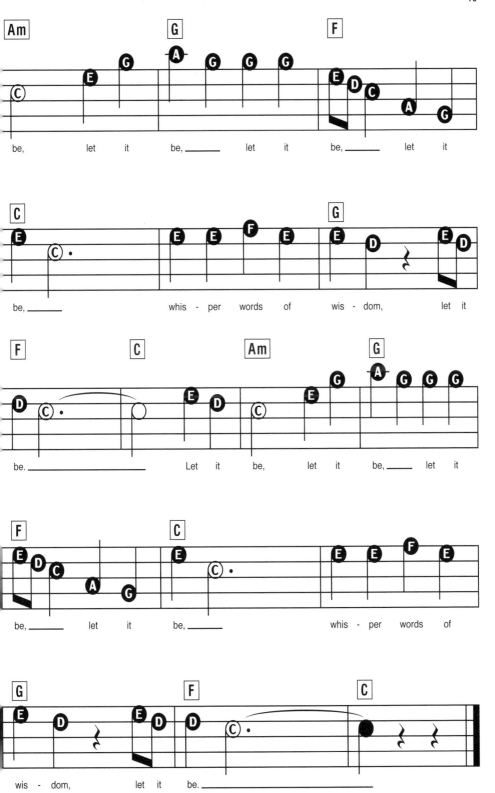

Long Ago
(And Far Away)
from COVER GIRL

Registration 3
Rhythm: Ballad or Swing

Words by Ira Gershwin
Music by Jerome Kern

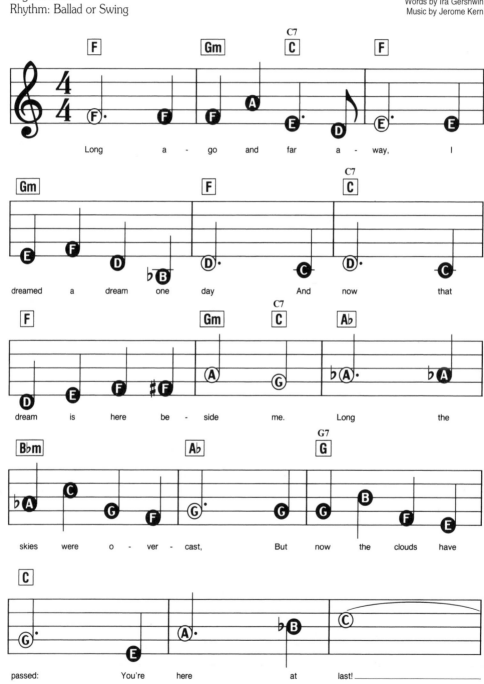

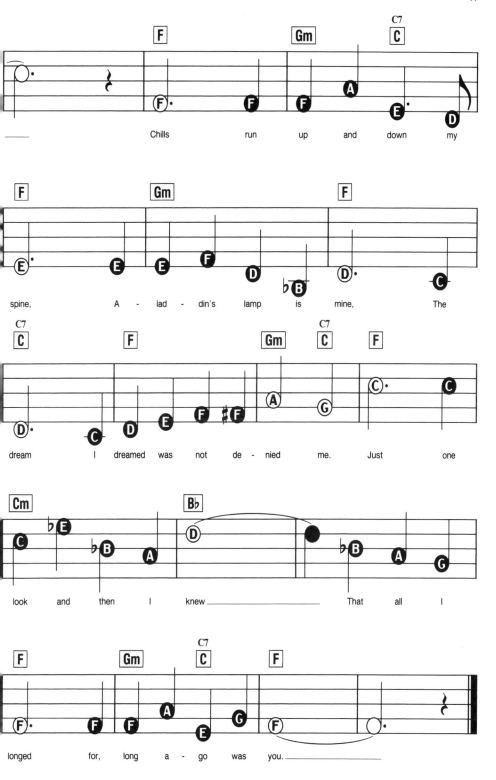

Love Me Tender

Registration 9
Rhythm: Slow Rock or Rock

Words and Music by Elvis Presley
and Vera Matson

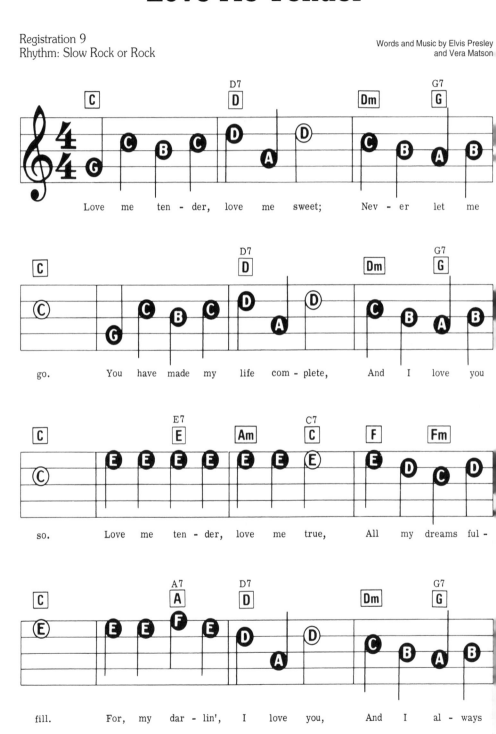

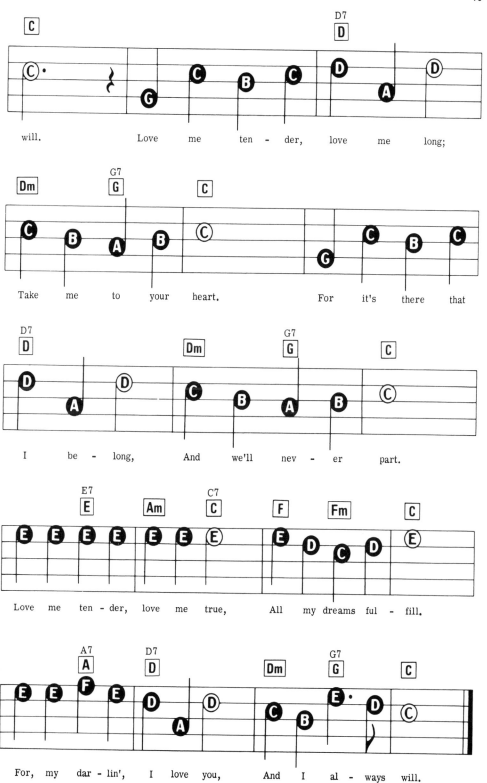

Love Walked In

Registration 9
Rhythm: Swing or Jazz

Music and Lyrics by George Gershwin
and Ira Gershwin

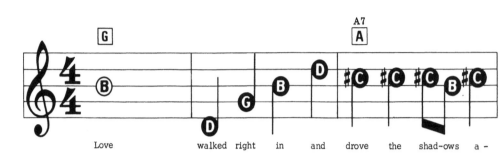

Love walked right in and drove the shad-ows a -

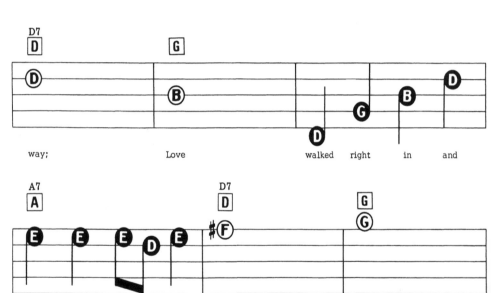

way; Love walked right in and

brought my sun - ni - est day. One

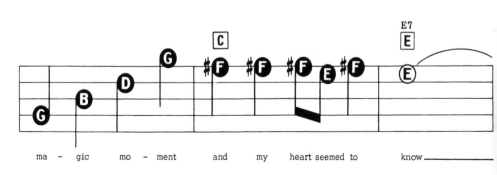

ma - gic mo - ment and my heart seemed to know

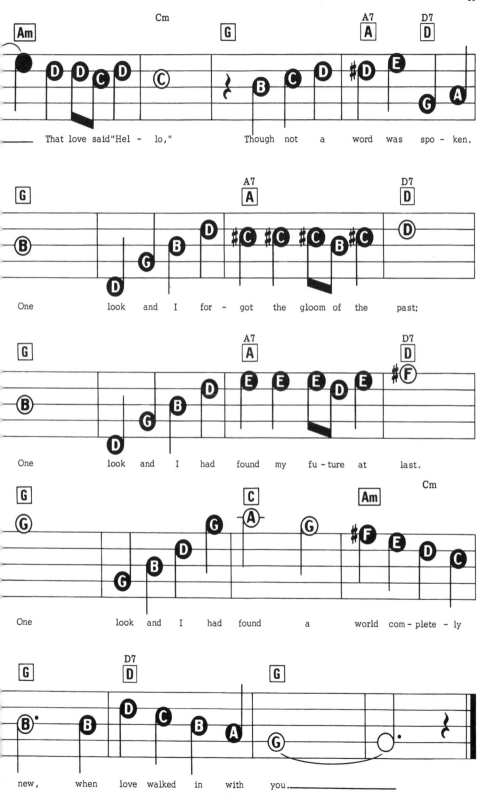

Memory
from CATS

Registration 3
Rhythm: 6/8 March

Music by Andrew Lloyd Webber
Text by Trevor Nunn after T.S. Eliot

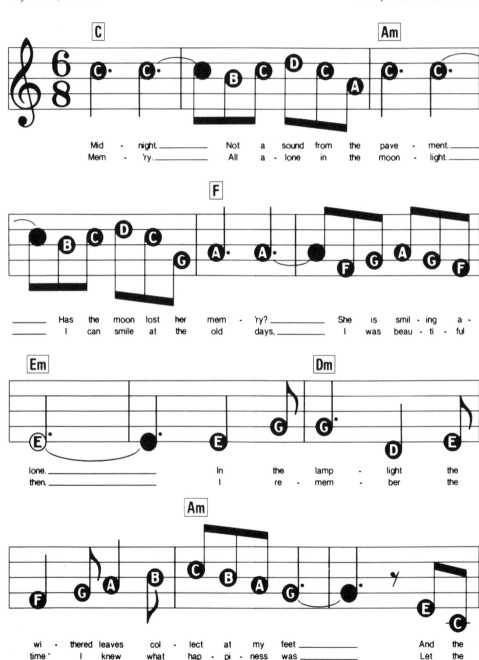

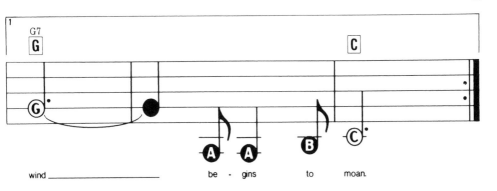

wind _____ be - gins to moan.

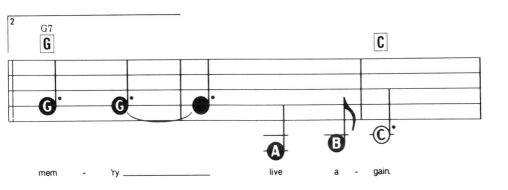

mem - 'ry _____ live a - gain.

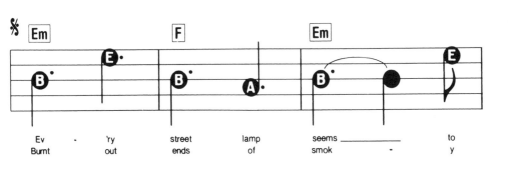

Ev - 'ry street lamp seems _____ to
Burnt out ends of smok - y

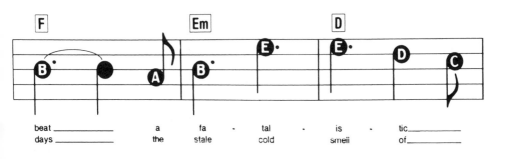

beat _____ a fa - tal - is - tic _____
days _____ the stale cold smell of _____

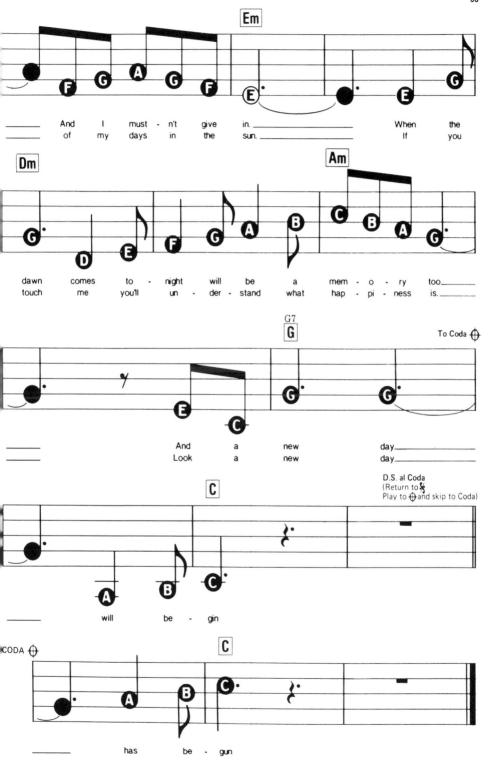

Mood Indigo

Registration 4
Rhythm: Swing or Ballad

Words and Music by Duke Ellington,
Irving Mills and Albany Bigard

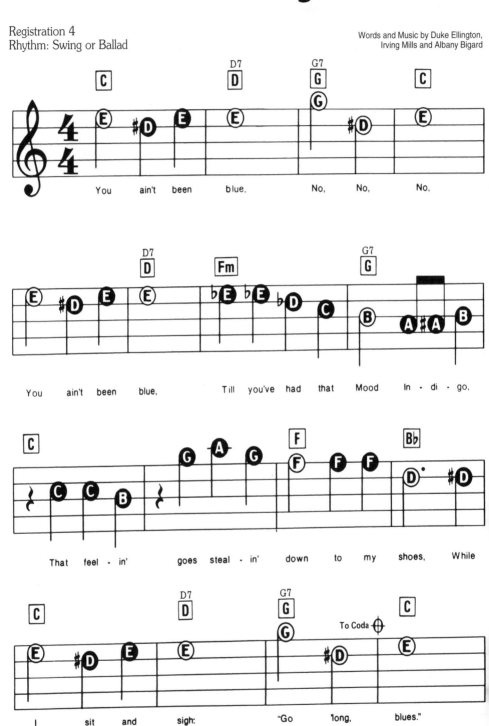

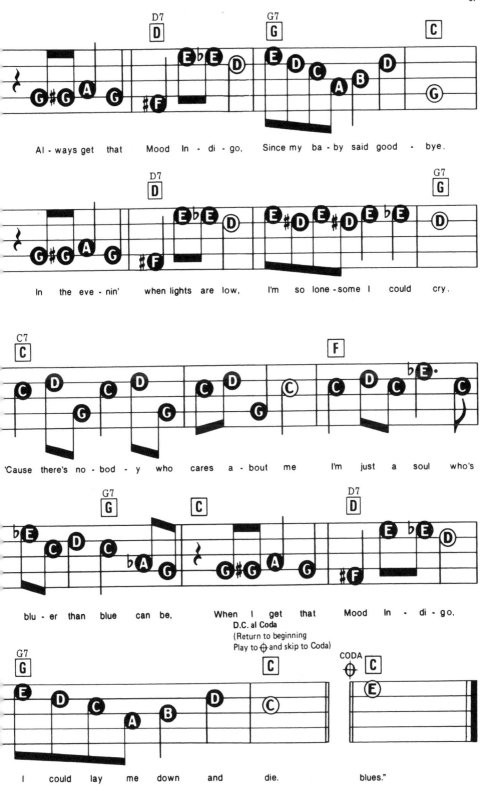

Moon River
from the Paramount Picture BREAKFAST AT TIFFANY'S

Registration 7
Rhythm: Waltz

Words by Johnny Mercer
Music by Henry Mancini

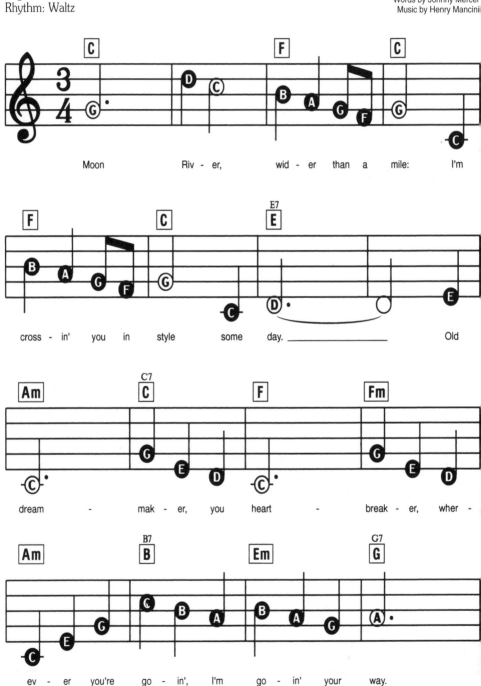

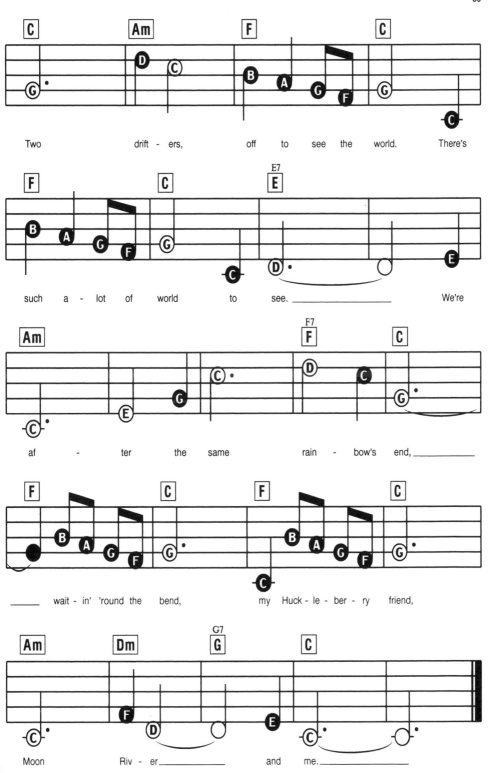

Moonlight in Vermont

Registration 2
Rhythm: Fox Trot or Swing

Words by John Blackburn
Music by Karl Suessdorf

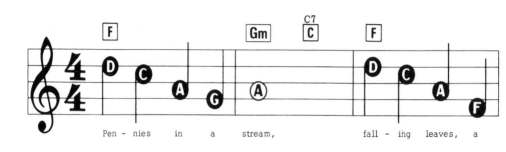

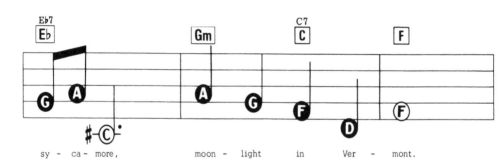

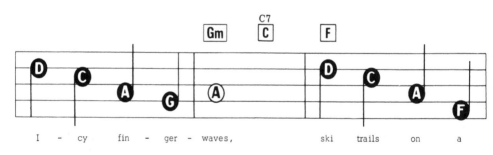

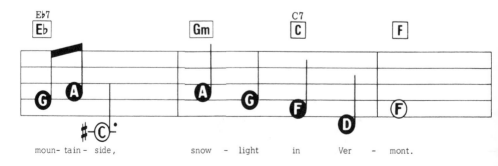

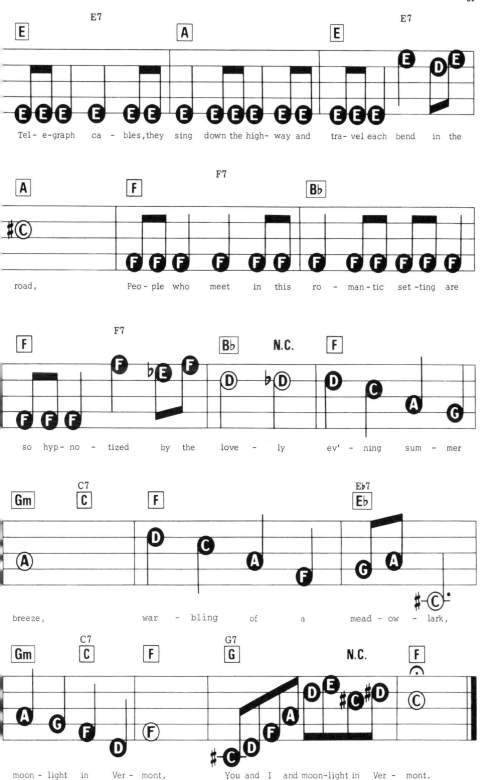

My Favorite Things
from THE SOUND OF MUSIC

Registration 9
Rhythm: Waltz

Lyrics by Oscar Hammerstein II
Music by Richard Rodgers

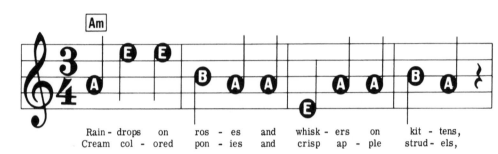

Rain - drops on ros - es and whisk - ers on kit - tens,
Cream col - ored pon - ies and crisp ap - ple strud - els,

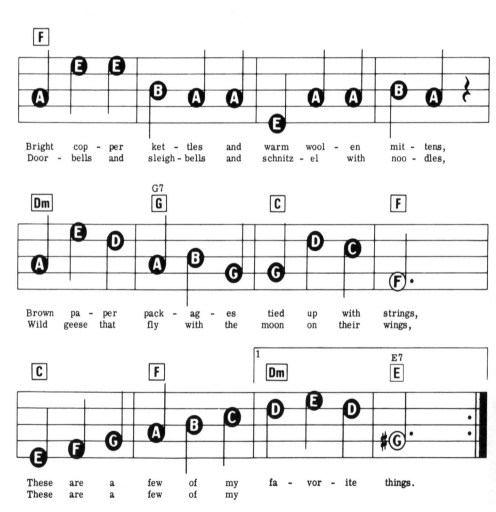

Bright cop - per ket - tles and warm wool - en mit - tens,
Door - bells and sleigh - bells and schnitz - el with noo - dles,

Brown pa - per pack - ag - es tied up with strings,
Wild geese that fly with the moon on their wings,

These are a few of my fa - vor - ite things.
These are a few of my

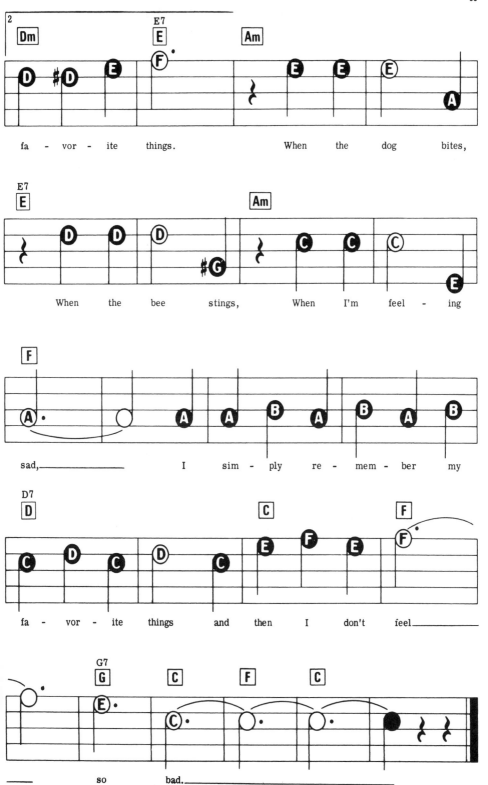

My Funny Valentine
from BABES IN ARMS

Registration 1
Rhythm: Ballad

Words by Lorenz Hart
Music by Richard Rodgers

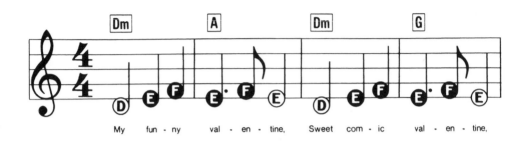

My fun - ny val - en - tine, Sweet com - ic val - en - tine,

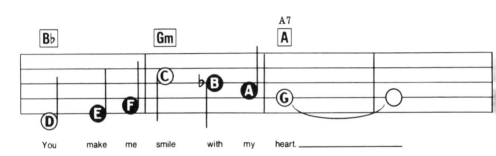

You make me smile with my heart.

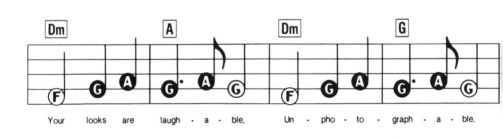

Your looks are laugh - a - ble, Un - pho - to - graph - a - ble,

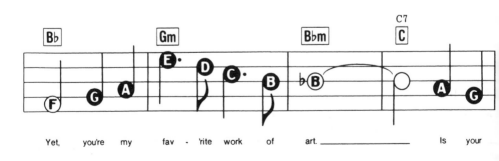

Yet, you're my fav - 'rite work of art. Is your

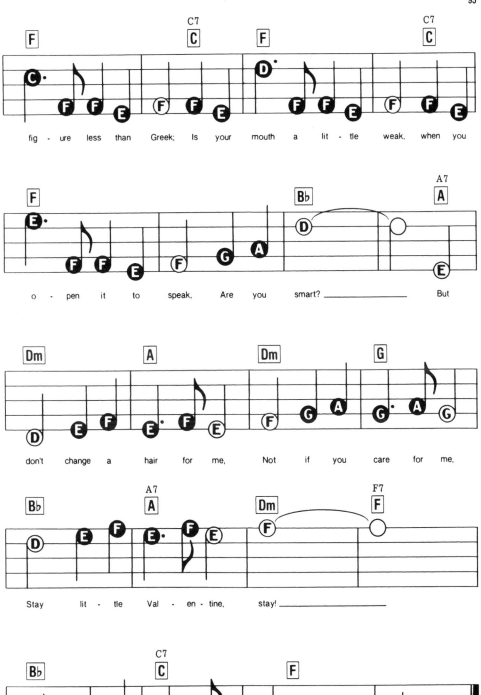

My Way

Registration 5
Rhythm: Ballad or Rock

English Words by Paul Anka
Original French Words by Gilles Thibault
Music by Jacques Revaux and Claude Francois

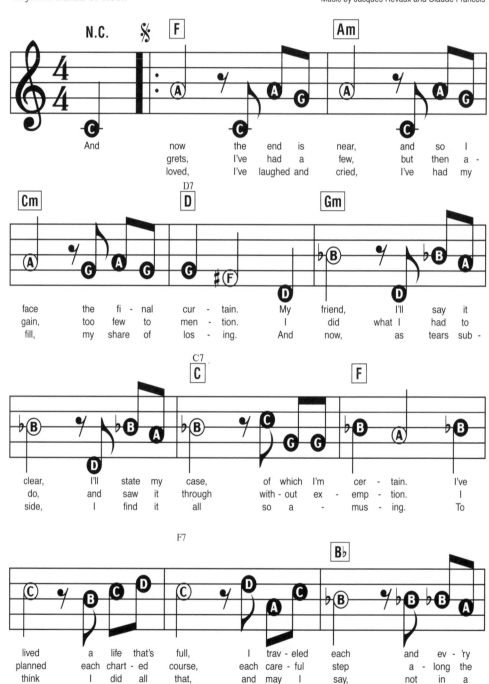

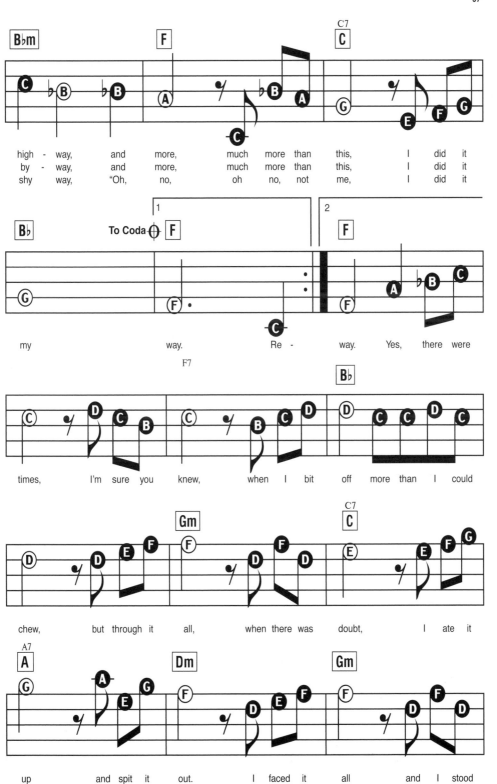

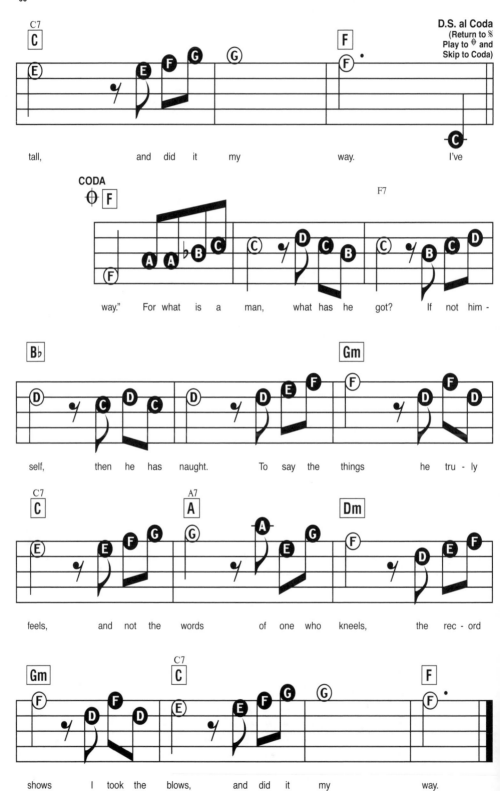

tall,　　　and did it my　　　way.　　　I've

way." For what is a man, what has he got? If not him -

self, then he has naught. To say the things he tru - ly

feels, and not the words of one who kneels, the rec - ord

shows I took the blows, and did it my way.

Over the Rainbow
from THE WIZARD OF OZ

Registration 5
Rhythm: Fox Trot or Swing

Music by Harold Arlen
Lyric by E.Y. "Yip" Harburg

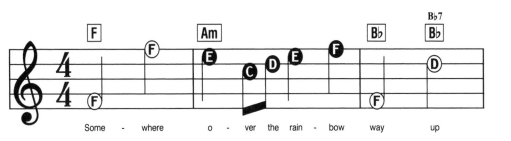

Some - where o - ver the rain - bow way up

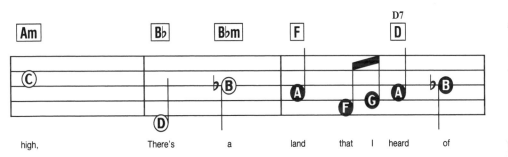

high, There's a land that I heard of

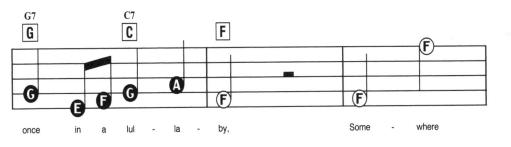

once in a lul - la - by, Some - where

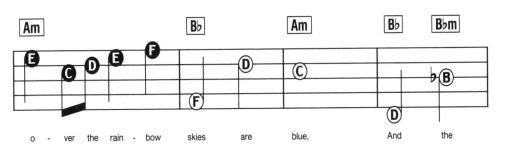

o - ver the rain - bow skies are blue, And the

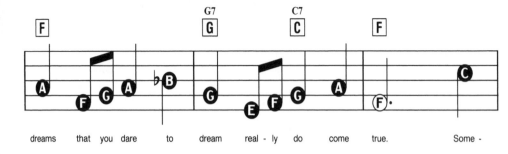

dreams   that you dare   to   dream   real - ly do   come   true.   Some -

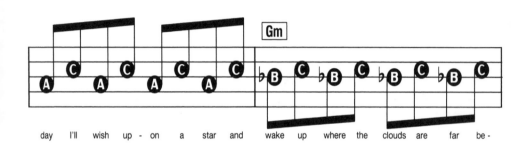

day   I'll wish up - on   a   star and   wake   up   where   the   clouds   are   far   be -

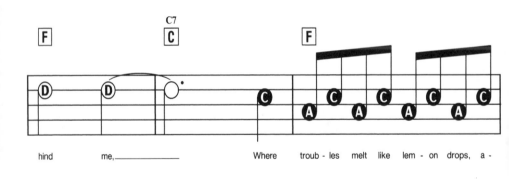

hind   me,_____   Where   troub - les   melt   like   lem - on   drops,   a -

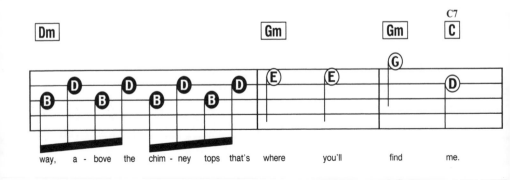

way,   a - bove   the   chim - ney   tops   that's   where   you'll   find   me.

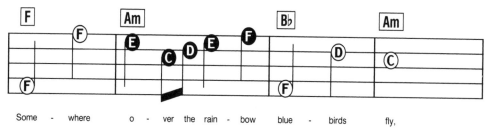

Some - where   o - ver the rain - bow   blue - birds   fly,

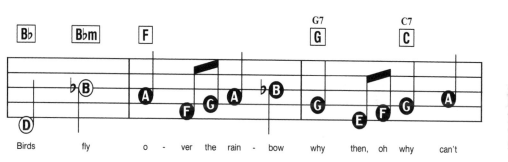

Birds   fly   o - ver the rain - bow   why   then, oh why   can't

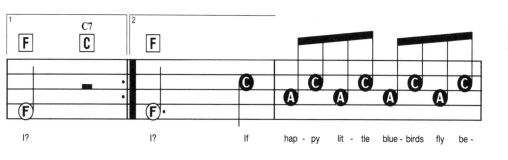

I?   I?   If   hap - py   lit - tle   blue - birds   fly   be-

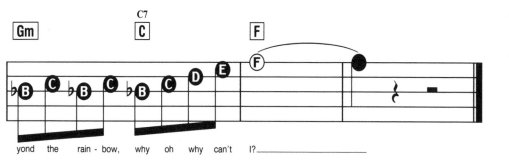

yond   the   rain - bow,   why   oh   why   can't   I?

Night and Day
from GAY DIVORCE

Registration 7
Rhythm: Fox Trot or Swing

Words and Music by
Cole Porter

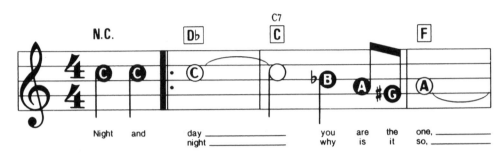

Night and day _____
night _____
you are the one, _____
why is it so, _____

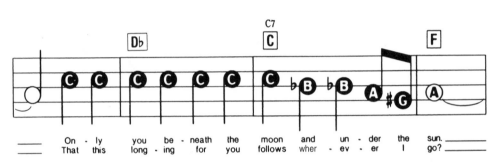

On - ly you be - neath the moon and un - der the sun. _____
That this long - ing for you follows wher - ev - er I go? _____

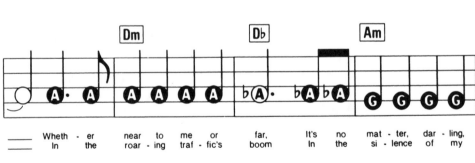

Wheth - er near to me or far, It's no mat - ter, dar - ling,
In the roar - ing traf - fic's boom In the si - lence of my

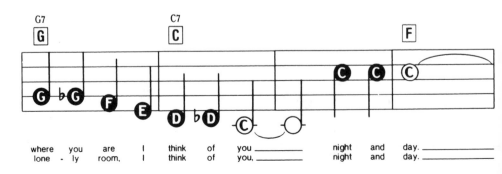

where you are I think of you _____ night and day. _____
lone - ly room, I think of you, _____ night and day. _____

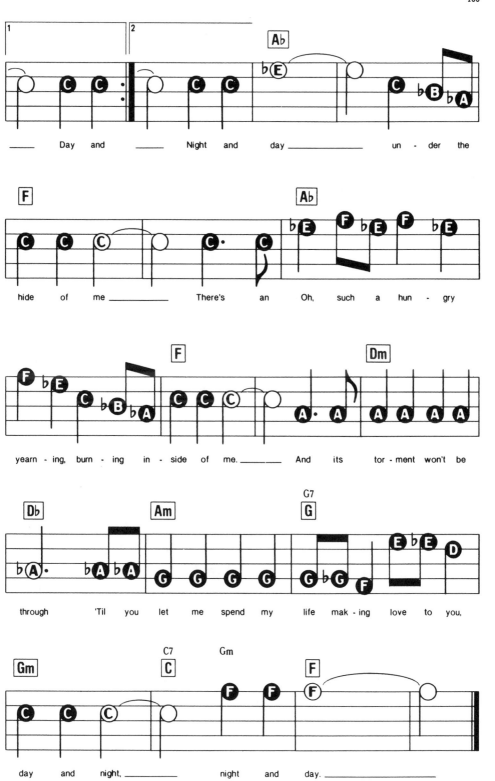

Ol' Man River
from SHOW BOAT

Registration 5
Rhythm: Ballad or Fox Trot

Lyrics by Oscar Hammerstein II
Music by Jerome Kern

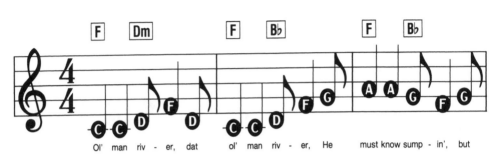

Ol' man riv - er, dat ol' man riv - er, He must know sump - in', but

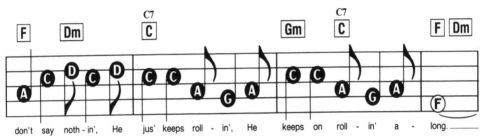

don't say noth - in', He jus' keeps roll - in', He keeps on roll - in' a - long.

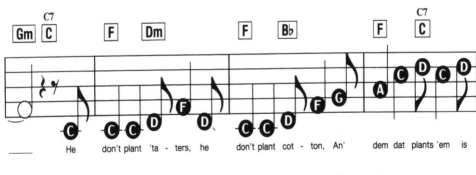

He don't plant 'ta - ters, he don't plant cot - ton, An' dem dat plants 'em is

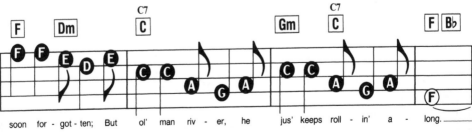

soon for - got - ten; But ol' man riv - er, he jus' keeps roll - in' a - long.

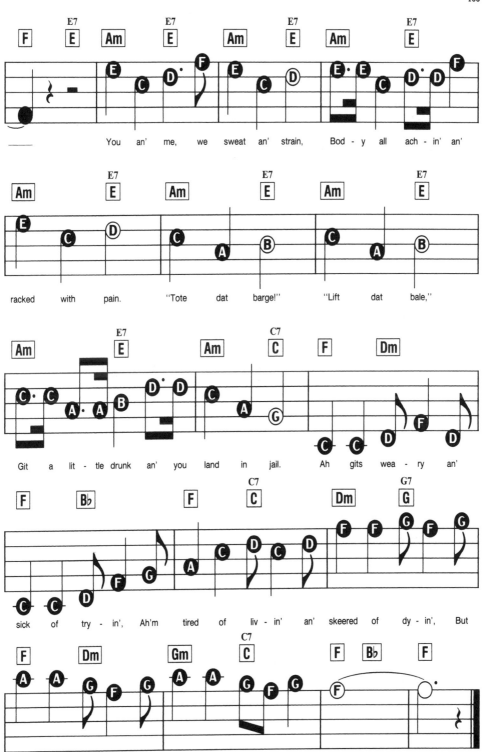

Piano Man

Registration 4
Rhythm: Waltz

Words and Music by
Billy Joel

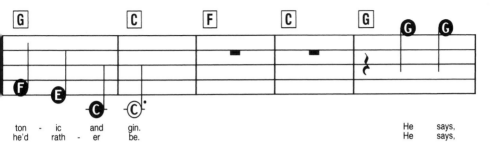

ton - ic and gin.   He says,
he'd rath - er be.   He says,

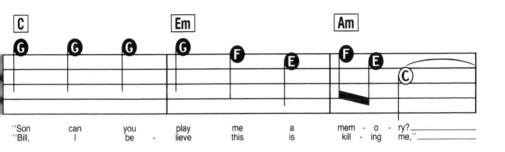

"Son can you play me a mem - o - ry?
"Bill, I be - lieve this is kill - ing me,"

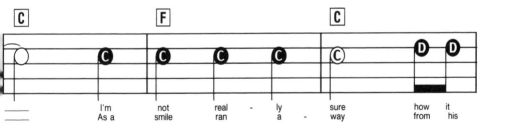

I'm not real - ly sure how it
As a smile ran a - way from his

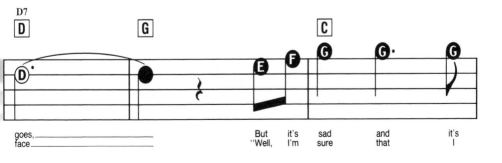

goes,
face

But it's sad and it's
"Well, I'm sure that I

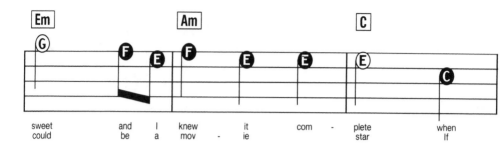

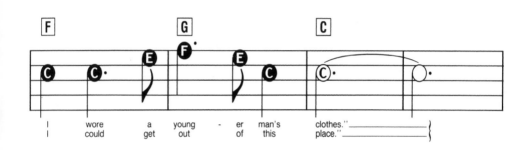

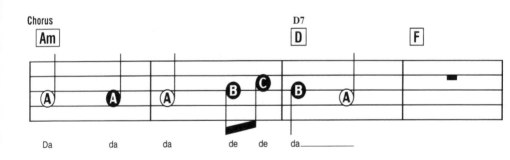

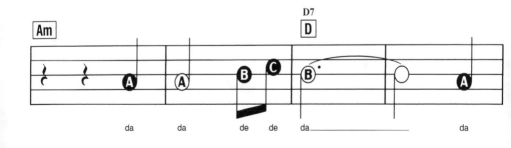

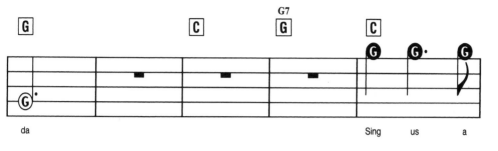

da   Sing   us   a

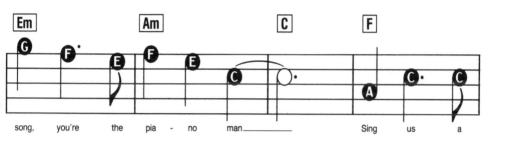

song,   you're   the   pia - no   man_____   Sing   us   a

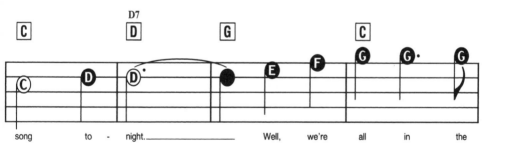

song   to - night._____   Well,   we're   all   in   the

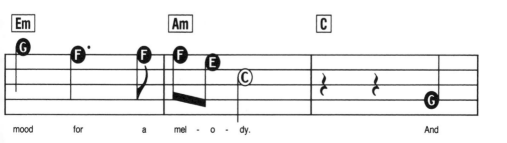

mood   for   a   mel - o - dy.   And

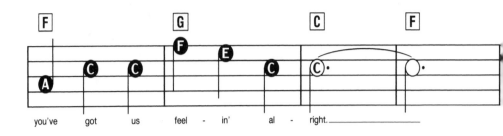

you've got us feel - in' al - right._____

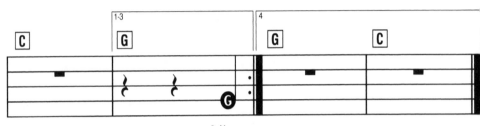

2. Now
3. Now

Additional Lyrics

3. Now Paul is a real estate novelist,
Who never had time for a wife,
And he's talkin' with Davey who's still in the Navy
And probably will be for life.
And the waitress is practicing politics,
As the businessmen slowly get stoned
Yes, they're sharing a drink they call loneliness
But it's better than drinkin' alone.

CHORUS

4. It's a pretty good crowd for a Saturday,
And the manager gives me a smile
'Cause he knows that it's me they've been comin' to see
To forget about life for a while.
And the piano sounds like a carnival
And the microphone smells like a beer
And they sit at the bar and put bread in my jar
And say "Man, what are you doin' here?"

CHORUS

Send in the Clowns
from the Musical A LITTLE NIGHT MUSIC

Registration 1
Rhythm: Slow Rock or Ballad

Words and Music by
Stephen Sondheim

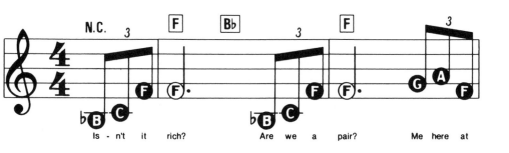

Is - n't it rich? Are we a pair? Me here at

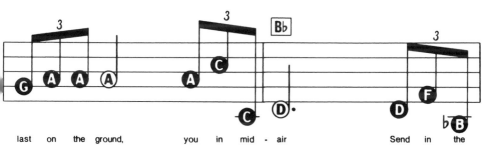

last on the ground, you in mid - air Send in the

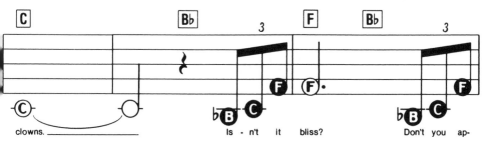

clowns. _____ Is - n't it bliss? Don't you ap-

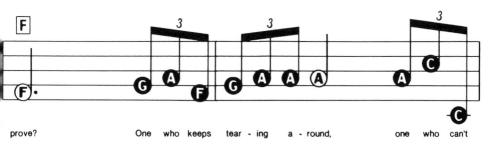

prove? One who keeps tear - ing a - round, one who can't

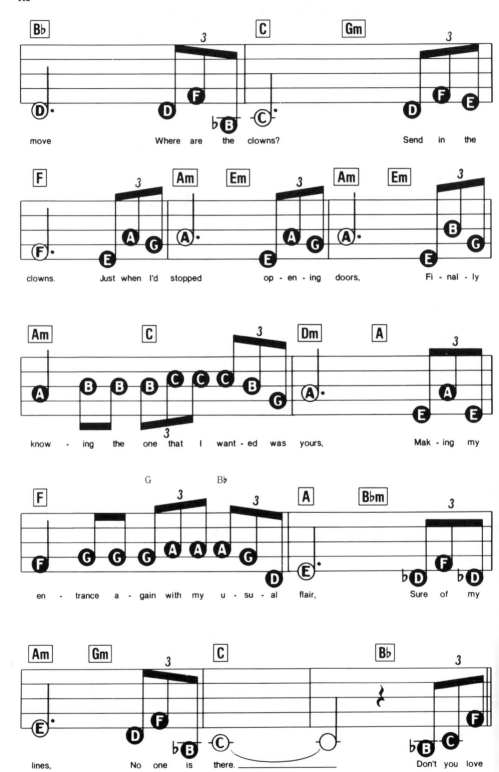

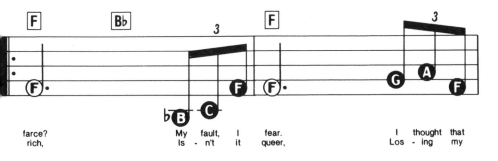

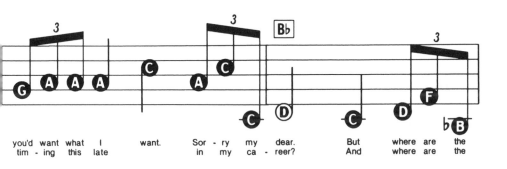

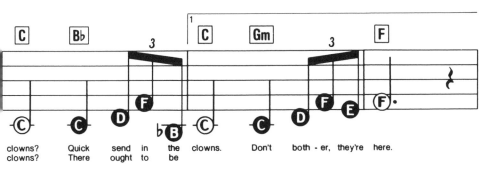

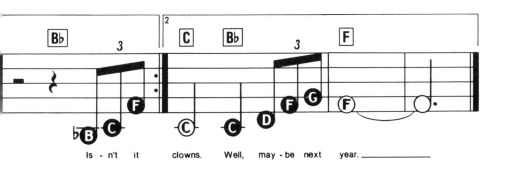

Satin Doll

from SOPHISTICATED LADIES

Registration 4
Rhythm: Swing or Jazz

Words by Johnny Mercer and Billy Strayhorn
Music by Duke Ellington

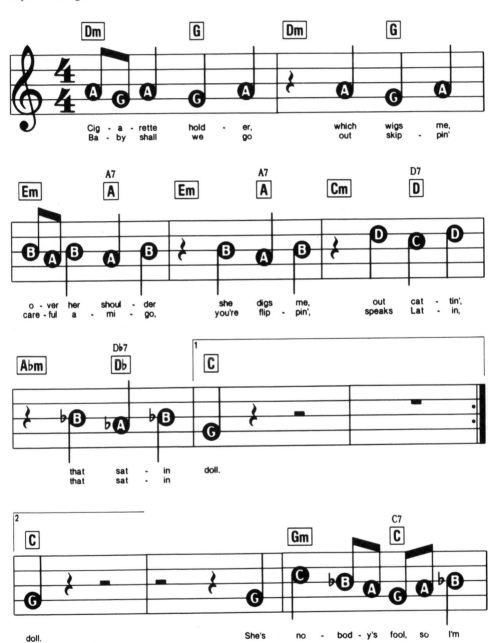

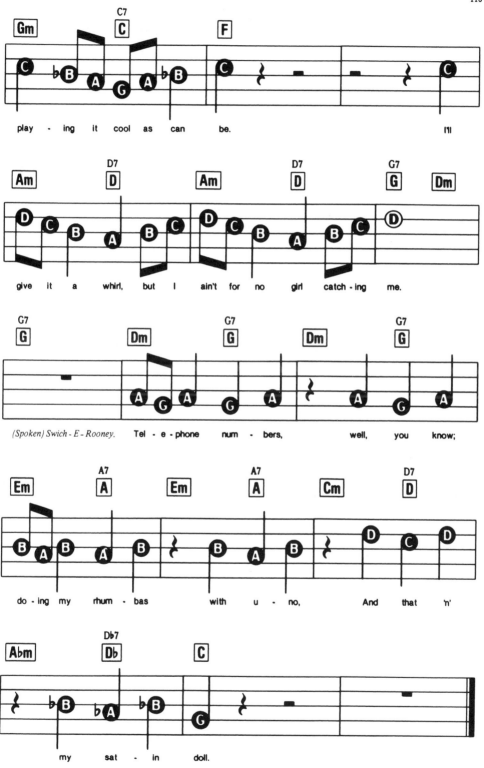

September Song
from the Musical KNICKERBOCKER HOLIDAY

Registration 2
Rhythm: Fox Trot

Words by Maxwell Anderson
Music by Kurt Weill

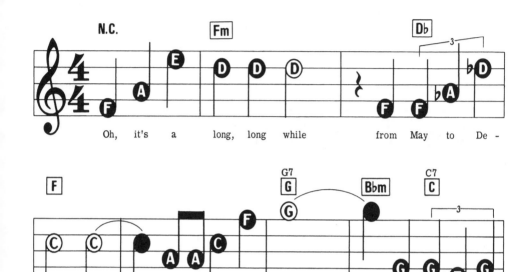

Oh, it's a long, long while from May to De -

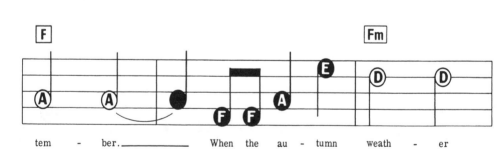

cem - ber,_____ But the days grow short,_____ when you reach Sep -

tem - ber._____ When the au - tumn weath - er

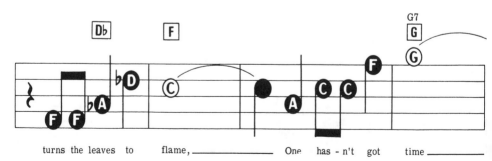

turns the leaves to flame,_____ One has - n't got time_____

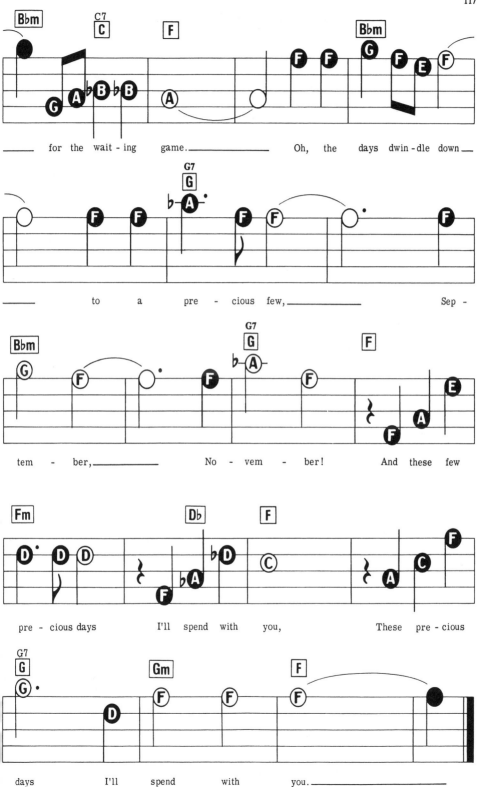

Skylark

Registration 3
Rhythm: Fox Trot or Swing

Words by Johnny Mercer
Music by Hoagy Carmichael

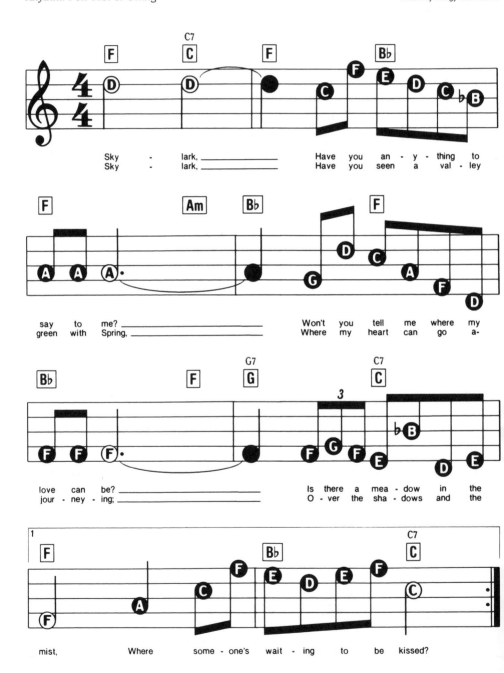

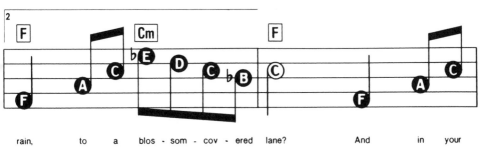

rain, to a blos - som - cov - ered lane? And in your

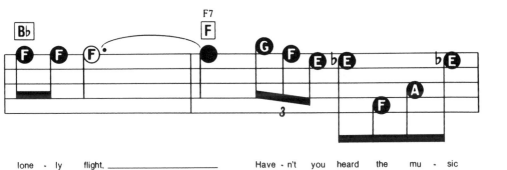

lone - ly flight, _____ Have - n't you heard the mu - sic

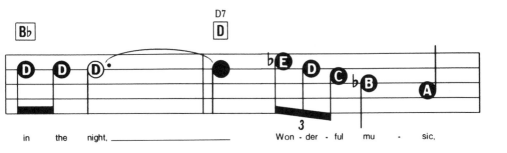

in the night, _____ Won - der - ful mu - sic,

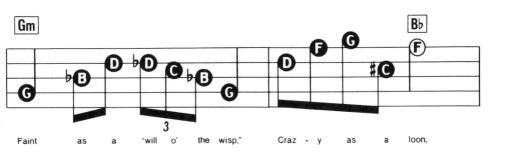

Faint as a "will o' the wisp," Craz - y as a loon,

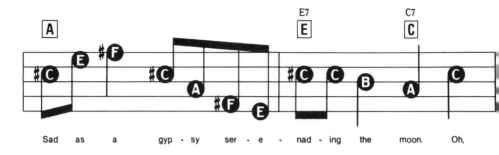

Sad as a gyp - sy ser - e - nad - ing the moon. Oh,

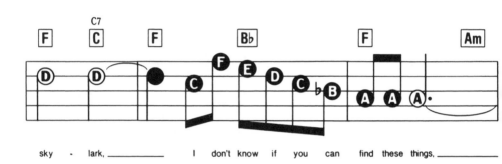

sky - lark, _____ I don't know if you can find these things, _____

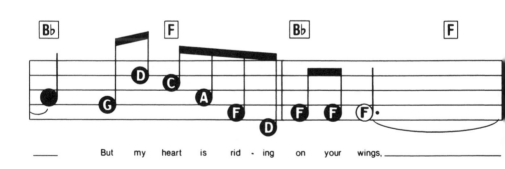

_____ But my heart is rid - ing on your wings, _____

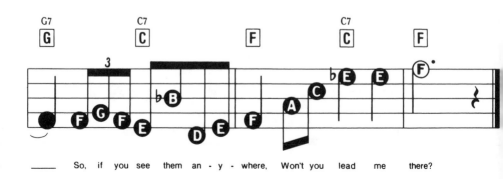

_____ So, if you see them an - y - where, Won't you lead me there?

Someone to Watch Over Me
from OH, KAY!

Registration 7
Rhythm: Ballad or Swing

Music and Lyrics by George Gershwin
and Ira Gershwin

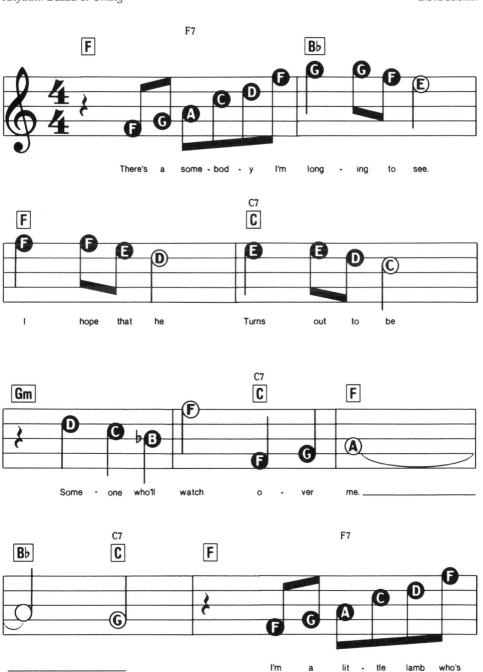

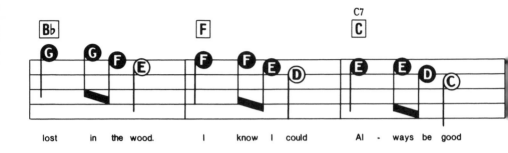

lost   in the wood.   I   know I could   Al - ways be good

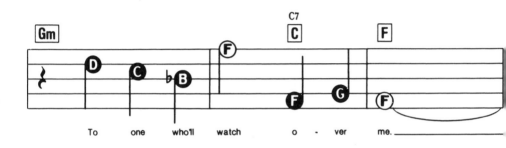

To   one   who'll   watch   o - ver   me.

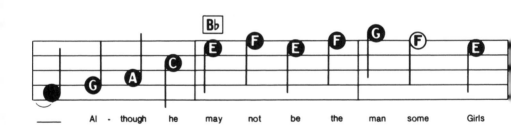

Al - though he may not be the man some Girls

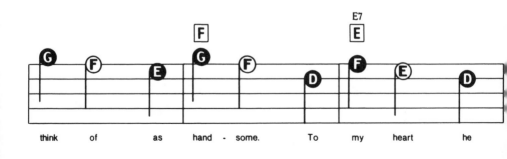

think   of   as hand - some.   To   my heart   he

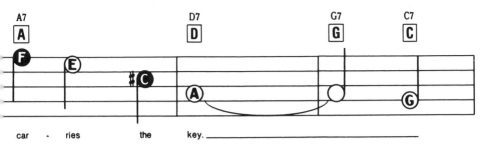

car - ries the key. _____

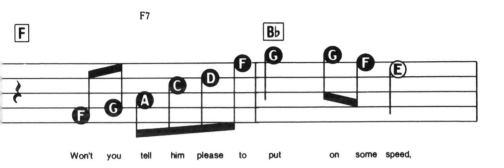

Won't you tell him please to put on some speed,

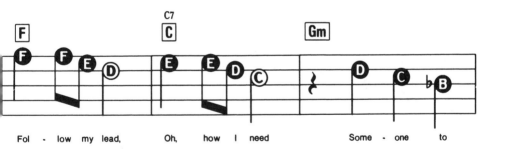

Fol - low my lead, Oh, how I need Some - one to

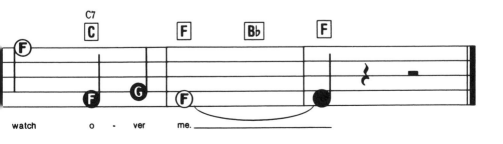

watch o - ver me. _____

Some Day My Prince Will Come

Registration 2
Rhythm: Waltz

Words by Larry Morey
Music by Frank Churchill

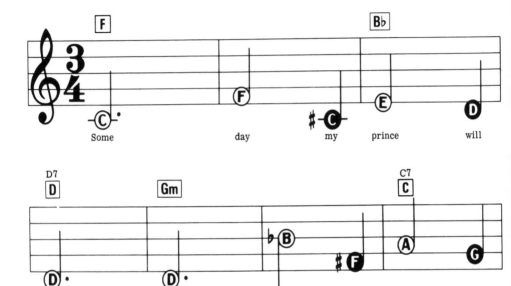

Some day my prince will

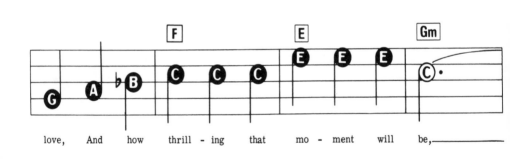

come, Some day I'll find my

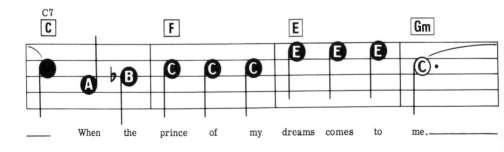

love, And how thrill - ing that mo - ment will be,____

When the prince of my dreams comes to me.____

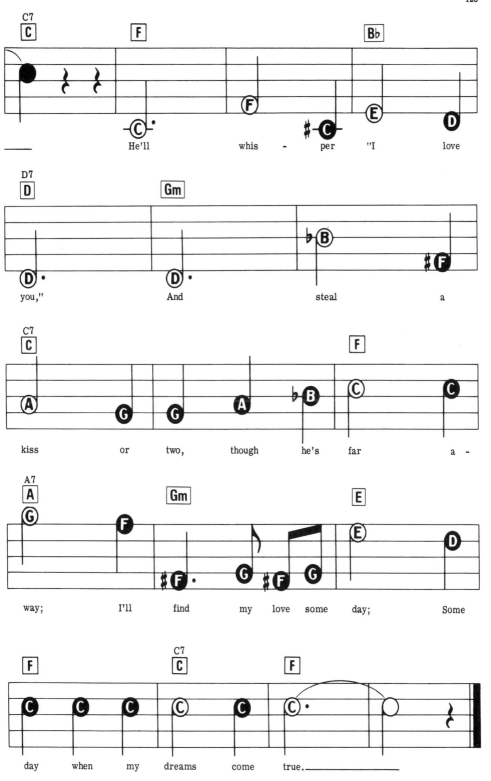

Somewhere
from WEST SIDE STORY

Registration 1
Rhythm: Slow Rock or Ballad

Lyrics by Stephen Sondheim
Music by Leonard Bernstein

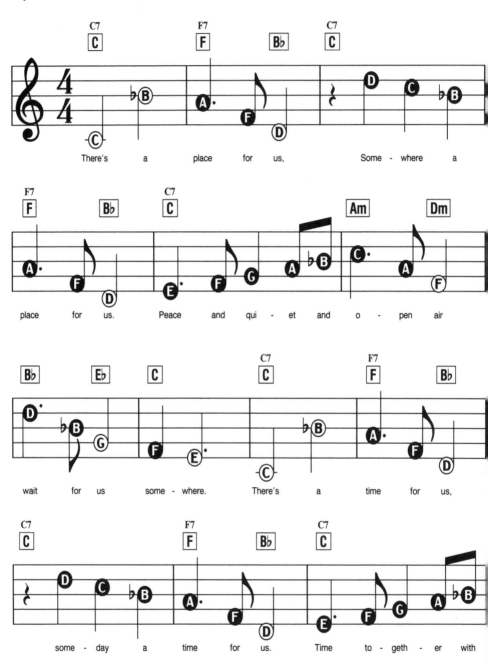

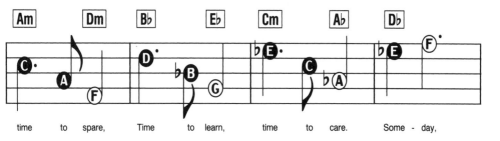

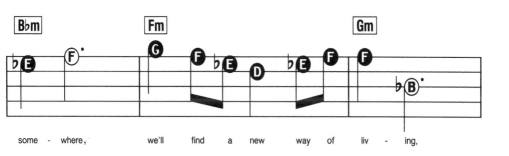

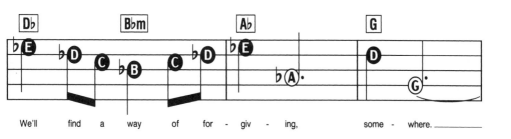

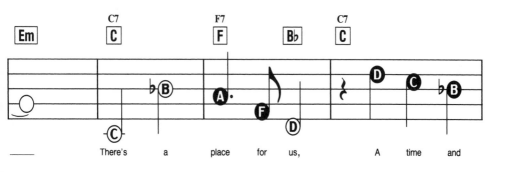

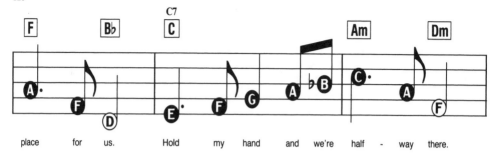

place   for   us.   Hold   my   hand   and   we're   half - way   there.

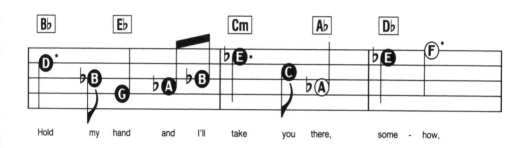

Hold   my   hand   and   I'll   take   you   there,   some - how,

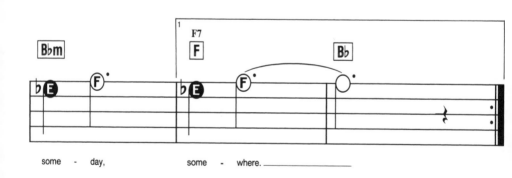

some - day,   some - where. _____

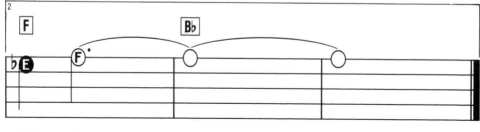

some - where. _____

Tears in Heaven

Registration 8
Rhythm: 8-Beat or Ballad

Words and Music by Eric Clapton
and Will Jennings

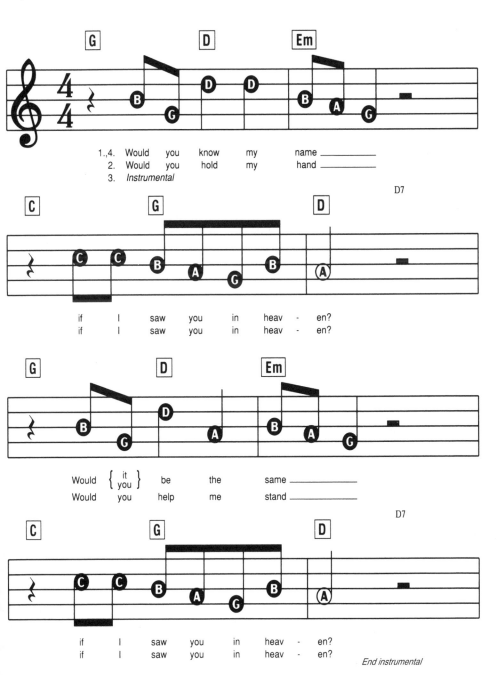

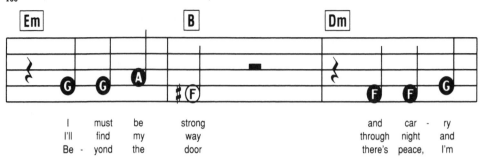

I	must	be	strong		and	car -	ry
I'll	find	my	way		through	night	and
Be -	yond	the	door		there's	peace,	I'm

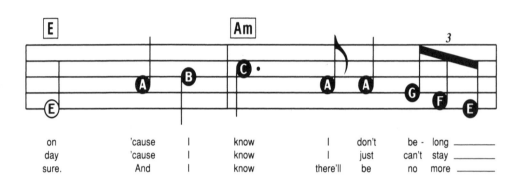

on	'cause	I	know	I	don't	be -	long _____
day	'cause	I	know	I	just	can't	stay _____
sure.	And	I	know	there'll	be	no	more _____

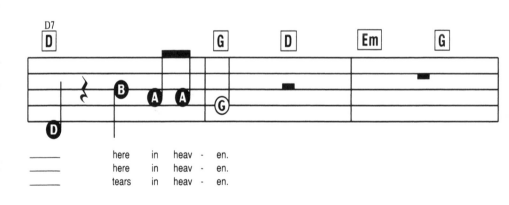

_____	here	in	heav -	en.
_____	here	in	heav -	en.
_____	tears	in	heav -	en.

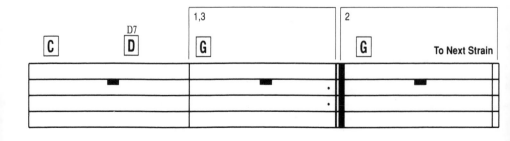

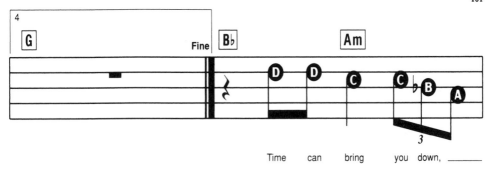

Time   can   bring   you   down, _____

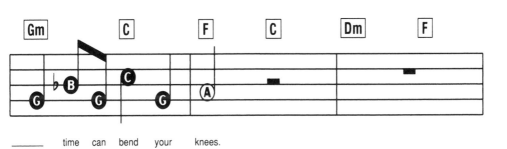

_____   time   can   bend   your   knees.

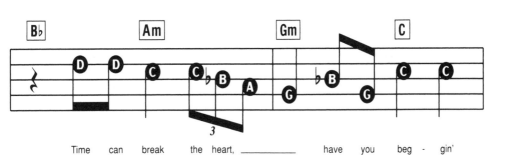

Time   can   break   the   heart, _____   have   you   beg - gin'

D.C. and Fade
(Return to beginning
and Fade)

D7

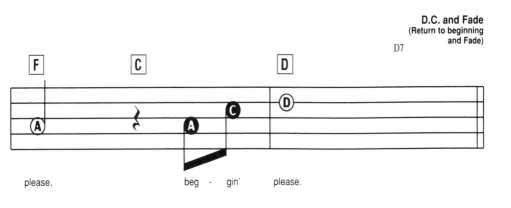

please,   beg - gin'   please.

Spanish Eyes

Registration 1
Rhythm: Latin

Words by Charles Singleton and Eddie Snyder
Music by Bert Kaempfert

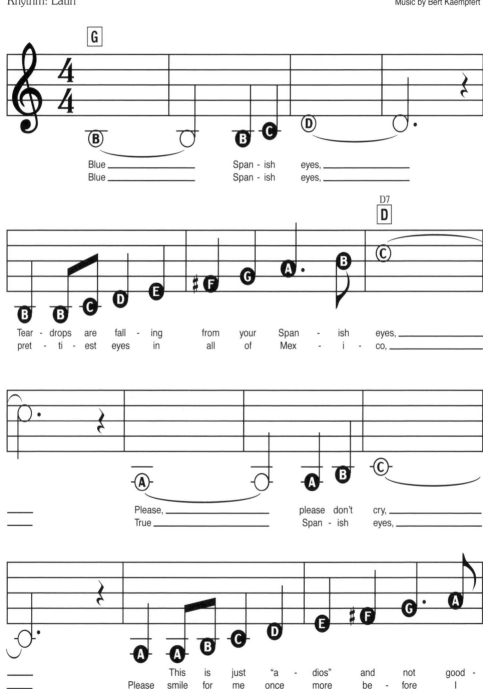

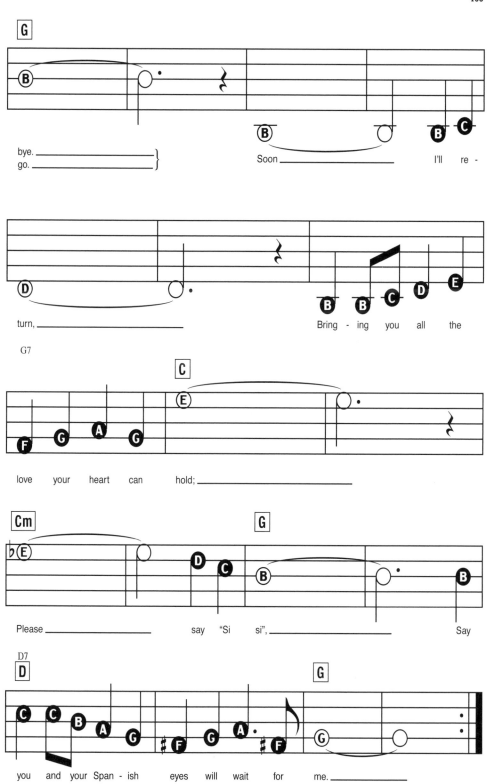

Speak Softly, Love
(Love Theme)
from the Paramount Picture THE GODFATHER

Registration 1
Rhythm: Ballad or Slow Rock

Words by Larry Kusik
Music by Nino Rota

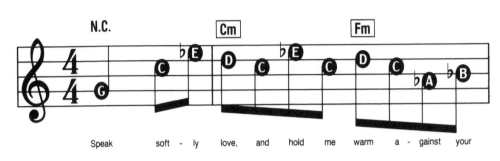

Speak soft - ly love, and hold me warm a - gainst your

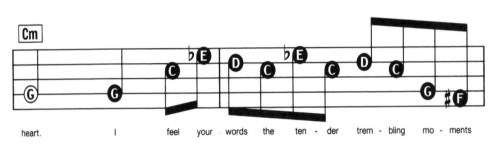

heart. I feel your words the ten - der trem - bling mo - ments

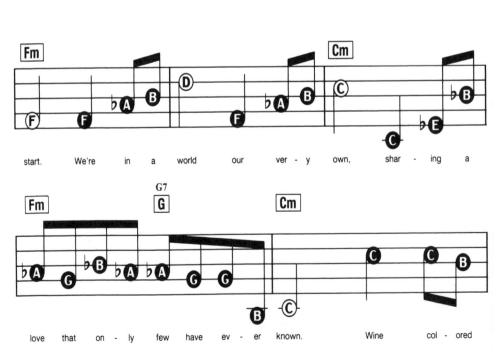

start. We're in a world our ver - y own, shar - ing a

love that on - ly few have ev - er known. Wine col - ored

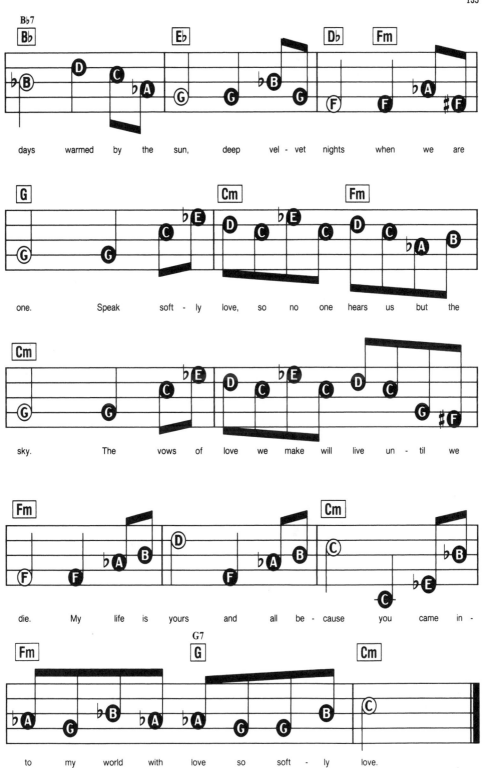

Stardust

Registration 5
Rhythm: Swing or Jazz

Words by Mitchell Parish
Music by Hoagy Carmichael

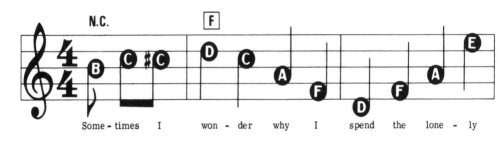

Some - times   I   won - der   why   I   spend   the   lone - ly

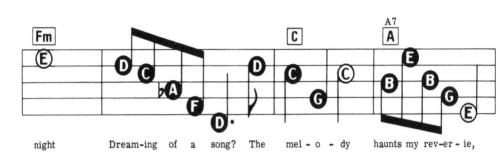

night   Dream-ing   of   a   song?   The   mel - o - dy   haunts my rev-er - ie,

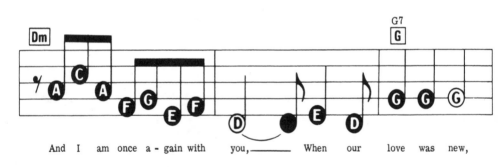

And   I   am once a - gain with   you,_____   When   our   love   was   new,

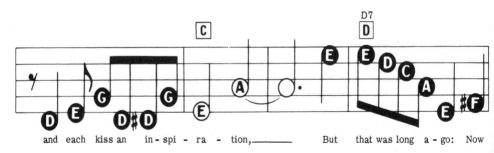

and   each   kiss   an   in - spi - ra - tion,_____   But   that was long a - go: Now

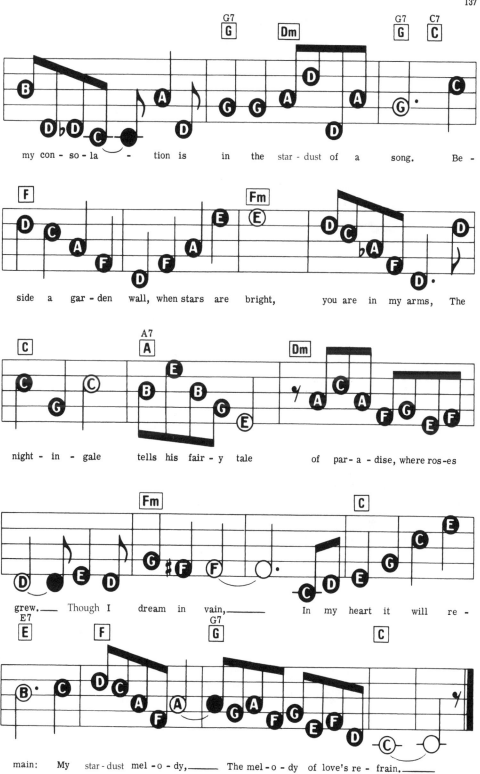

Stormy Weather

(Keeps Rainin' All the Time)
from COTTON CLUB PARADE OF 1933

Registration 2
Rhythm: Ballad or R&B

Lyric by Ted Koehler
Music by Harold Arlen

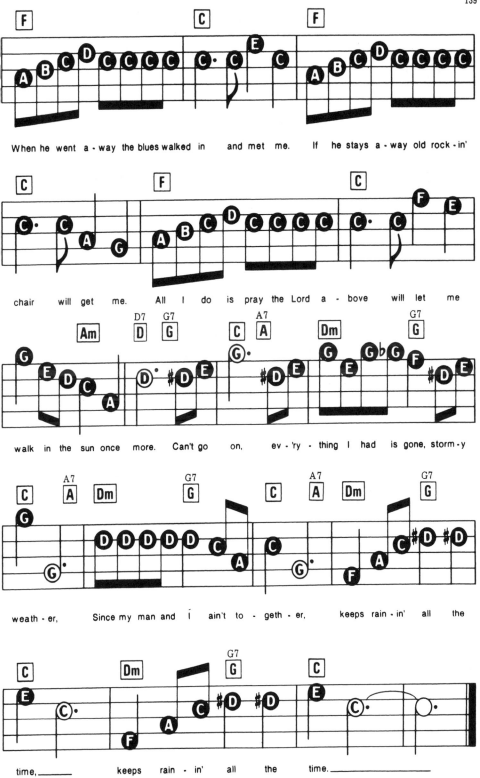

Summertime
from PORGY AND BESS®

Registration 10
Rhythm: Ballad or Blues

Music and Lyrics by George Gershwin,
DuBose and Dorothy Heyward
and Ira Gershwin

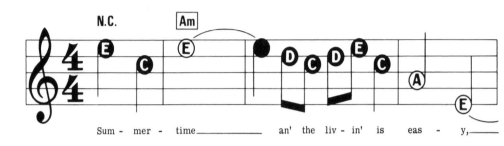

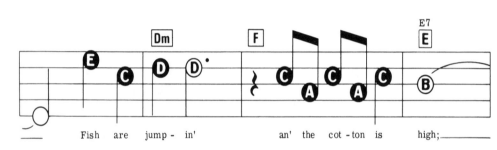

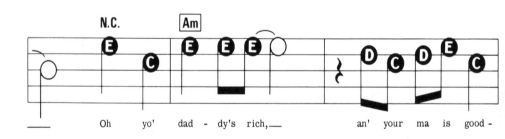

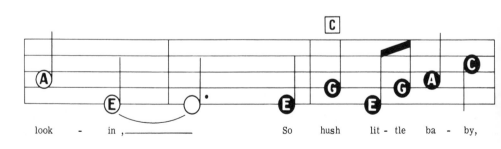

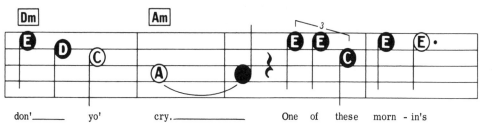

don'_____ yo' cry._____ One of these morn - in's

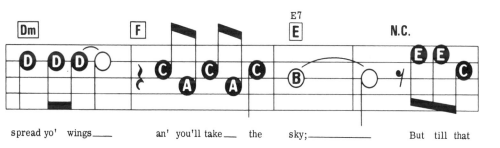

you goin' to rise___ up sing - in',_____ Then you'll

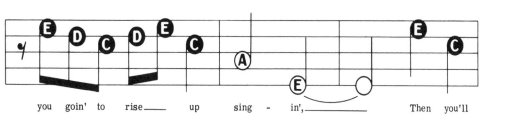

spread yo' wings___ an' you'll take___ the sky;_____ But till that

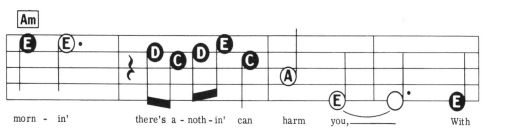

morn - in' there's a - noth - in' can harm you,_____ With

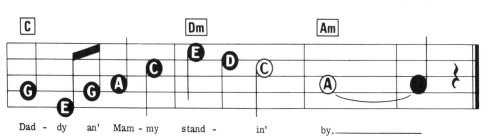

Dad - dy an' Mam - my stand - in' by._____

They Can't Take That Away from Me

from THE BARKLEYS OF BROADWAY

Registration 1
Rhythm: Ballad or Fox Trot

Music and Lyrics by George Gershwin
and Ira Gershwin

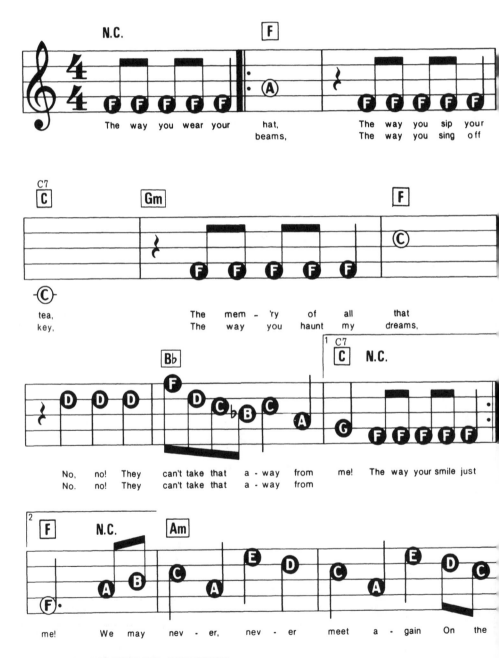

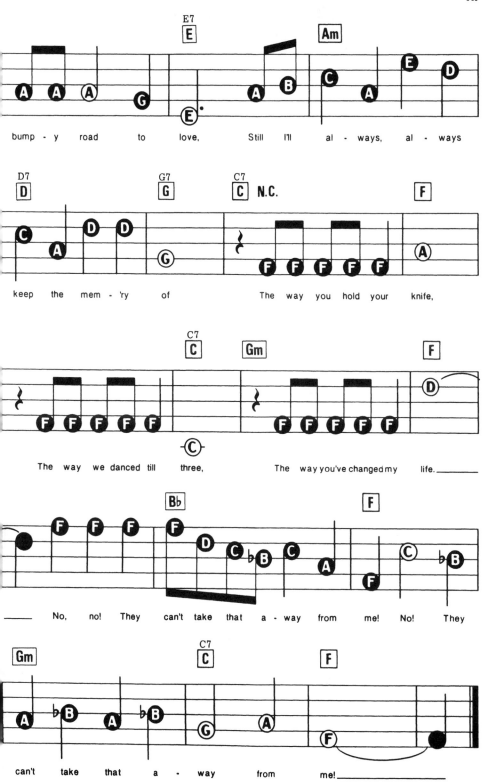

A Time for Us
(Love Theme)
from the Paramount Picture ROMEO AND JULIET

Registration 1
Rhythm: Waltz

Words by Larry Kusik and Eddie Snyder
Music by Nino Rota

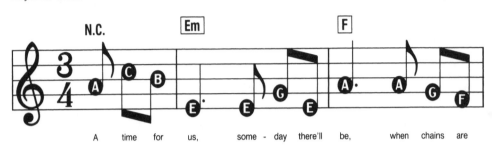

A   time   for   us,   some - day there'll be,   when chains are

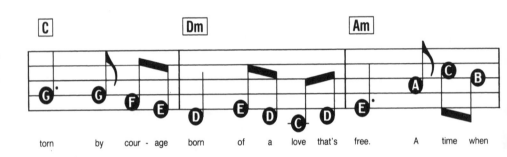

torn   by   cour - age   born   of   a   love that's free.   A   time when

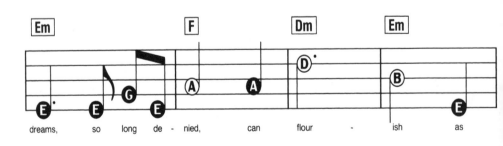

dreams,   so   long   de - nied,   can   flour - ish   as

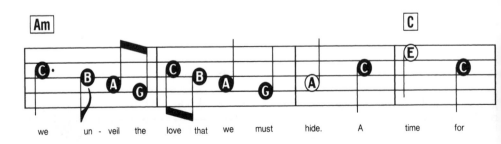

we   un - veil   the   love   that we   must   hide.   A   time   for

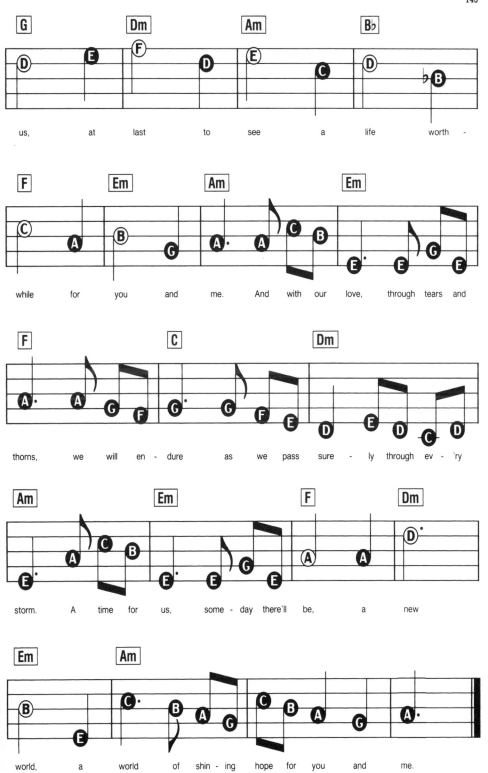

Top of the World

Registration 2
Rhythm: Fox Trot

Words and Music by John Bettis
and Richard Carpenter

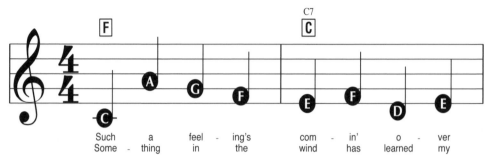

Such a feel - ing's com - in' o - ver
Some - thing in the wind has learned my

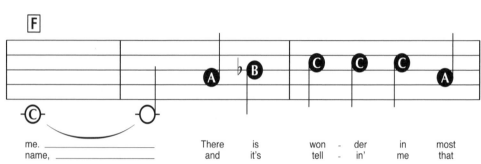

me. _____ There is won - der in most
name, _____ and it's tell - in' me that

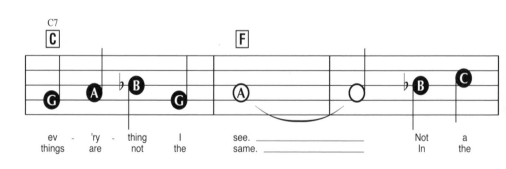

ev - 'ry - thing I see. _____ Not a
things are not the same. _____ In the

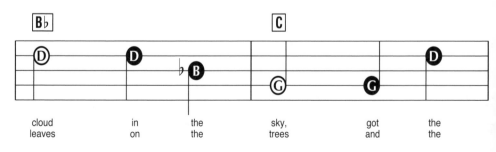

cloud in the sky, got the
leaves on the trees and the

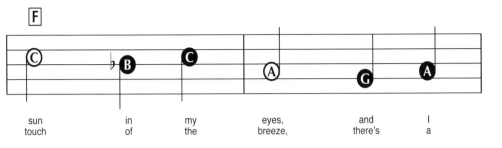

sun | in | my | eyes, | and | I
touch | of | the | breeze, | there's | a

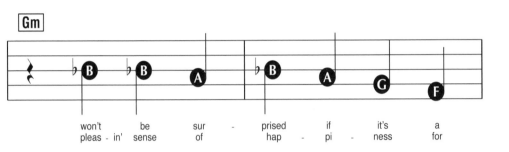

won't | be | sur | - | prised | if | it's | a
pleas - in' | sense | of | | hap | - pi | - ness | for

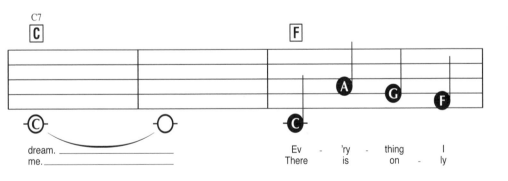

dream. | | Ev | - 'ry | - thing | I
me. | | There | is | on | - ly

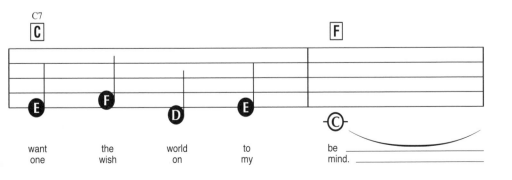

want | the | world | to | be
one | wish | on | my | mind.

148

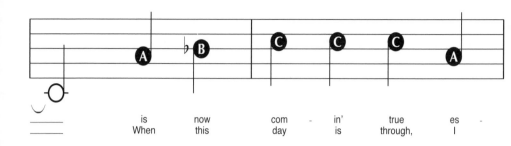

is now com - in' true es -
When this day is through, I

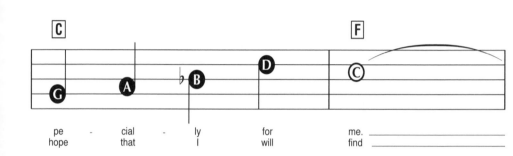

pe - cial - ly for me. _____
hope that I will find _____

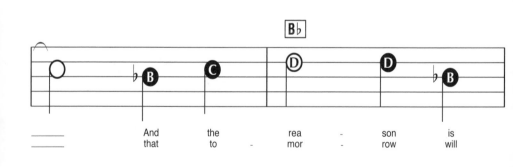

_____ And the rea - son is
_____ that to - mor - row will

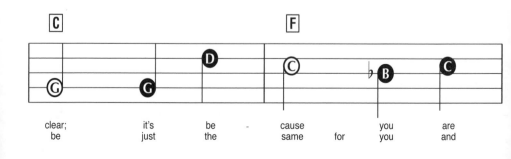

clear; it's be - cause you are
be just the same for you and

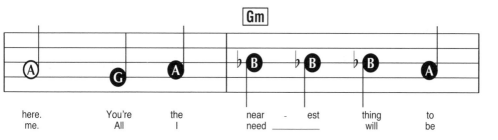

here. You're the near - est thing to
me. All I need will be

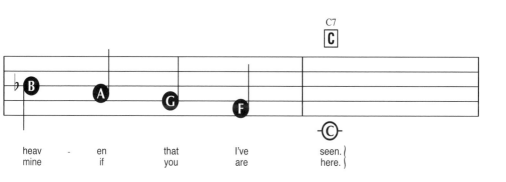

heav - en that I've seen.
mine if you are here.

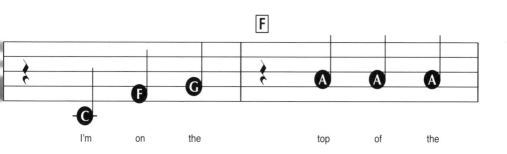

I'm on the top of the

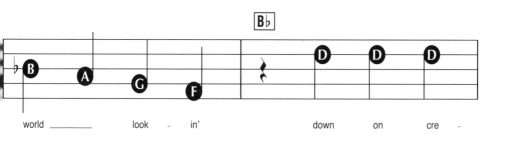

world look - in' down on cre -

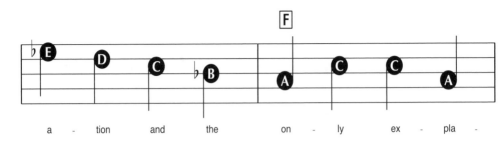

a - tion and the on - ly ex - pla -

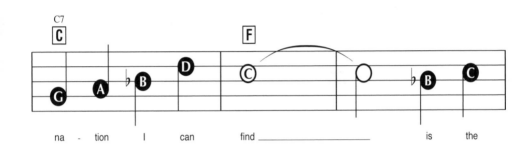

na - tion I can find _____ is the

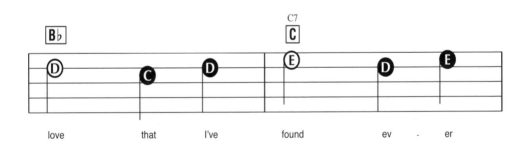

love that I've found ev - er

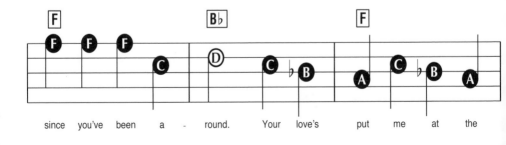

since you've been a - round. Your love's put me at the

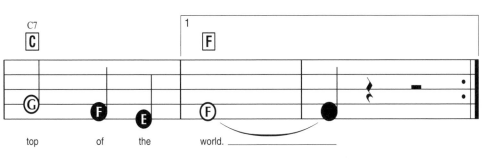

top   of   the   world.

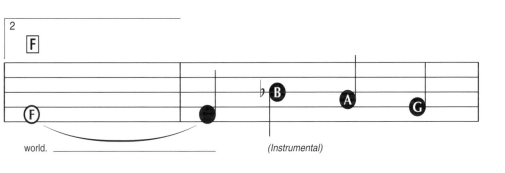

world. _____ _(Instrumental)_

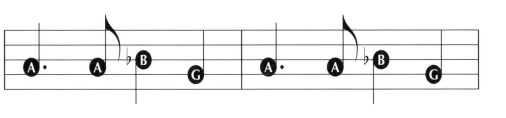

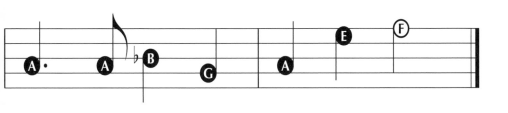

Unchained Melody

Registration 4
Rhythm: Ballad

Lyric by Hy Zaret
Music by Alex North

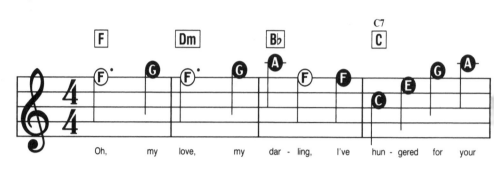

Oh, my love, my dar - ling, I've hun - gered for your

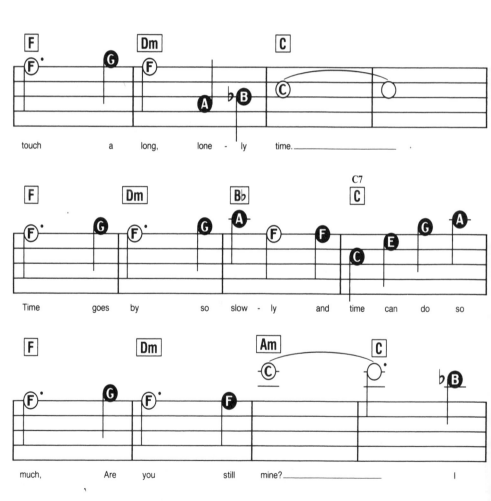

touch a long, lone - ly time.

Time goes by so slow - ly and time can do so

much, Are you still mine?

Unforgettable

Registration 3
Rhythm: Fox Trot or Swing

Words and Music by
Irving Gordon

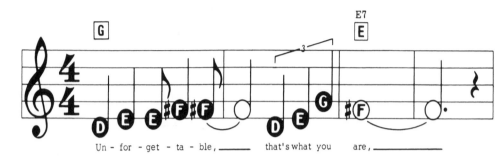

Un - for - get - ta - ble, _____ that's what you are, _____

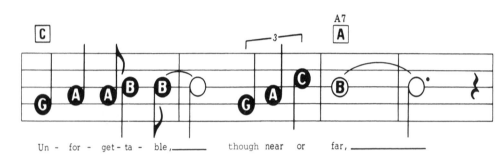

Un - for - get - ta - ble, _____ though near or far, _____

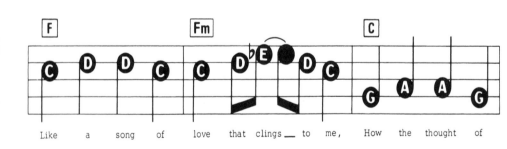

Like a song of love that clings _ to me, How the thought of

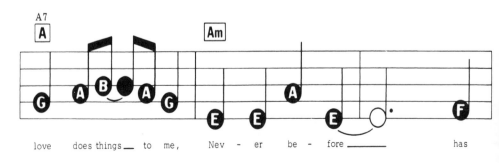

love does things _ to me, Nev - er be - fore _____ has

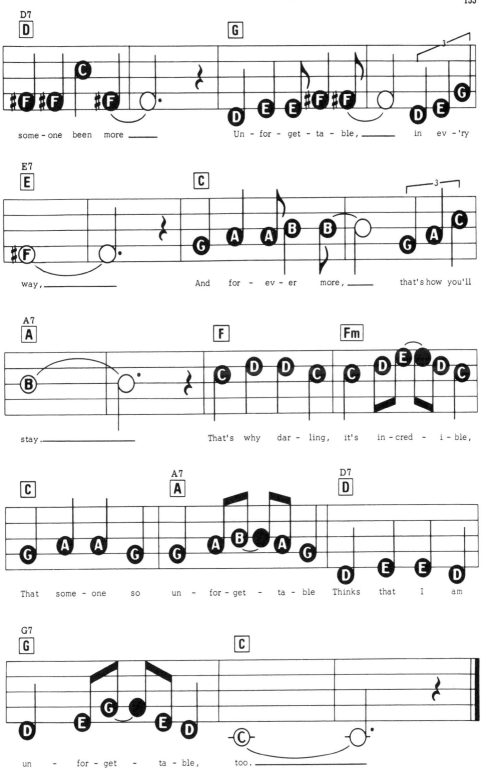

The Very Thought of You

Registration 8
Rhythm: Ballad or Fox Trot

Words and Music by
Ray Noble

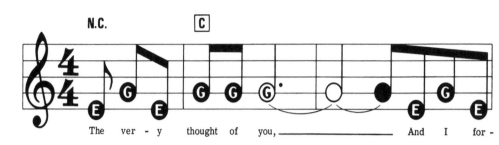

The ver - y thought of you, _____ And I for -

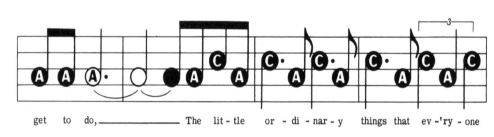

get to do, _____ The lit - tle or - di - nar - y things that ev - 'ry - one

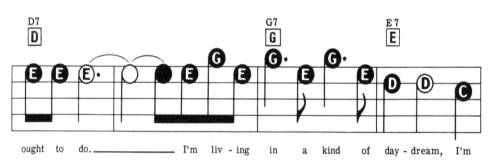

ought to do. _____ I'm liv - ing in a kind of day - dream, I'm

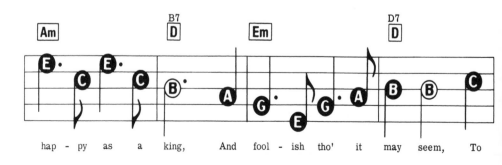

hap - py as a king, And fool - ish tho' it may seem, To

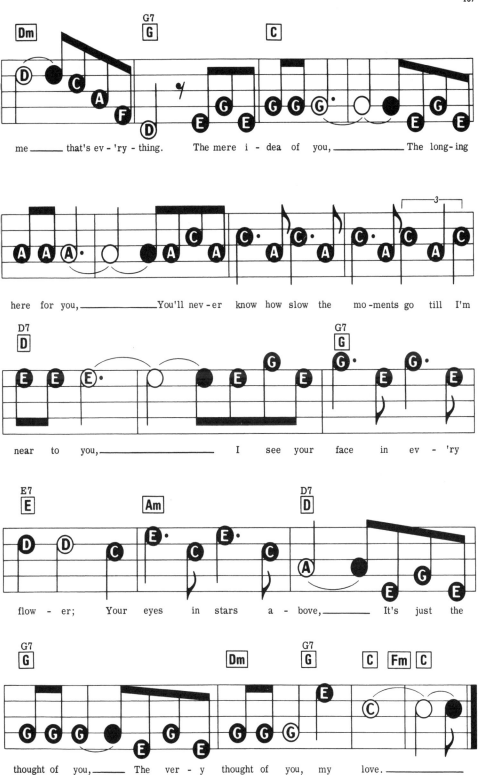

me ____ that's ev - 'ry - thing. The mere i - dea of you, ____ The long- ing

here for you, ____ You'll nev - er know how slow the mo -ments go till I'm

near to you, ____ I see your face in ev - 'ry

flow - er; Your eyes in stars a - bove, ____ It's just the

thought of you, ____ The ver - y thought of you, my love. ____

We've Only Just Begun

Registration 1
Rhythm: 8-Beat or Pops

Words and Music by Roger Nichols
and Paul Williams

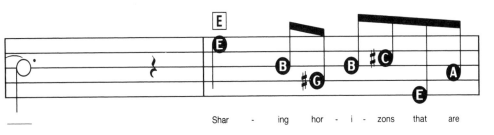

Shar - ing hor - i - zons that are

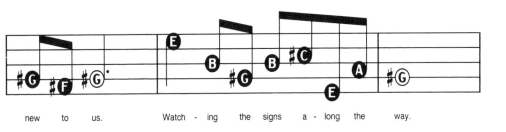

new to us. Watch - ing the signs a - long the way.

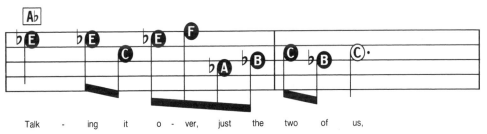

Talk - ing it o - ver, just the two of us,

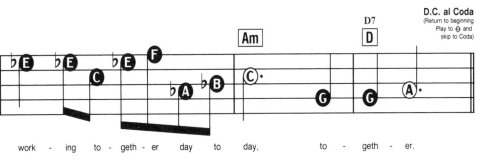

work - ing to - geth - er day to day, to - geth - er.

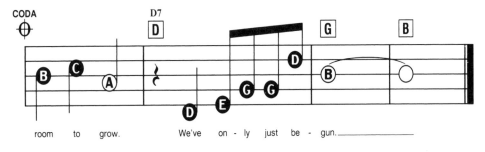

room to grow. We've on - ly just be - gun.

What a Wonderful World

Registration 2
Rhythm: Ballad

Words and Music by George David Weiss
and Bob Thiele

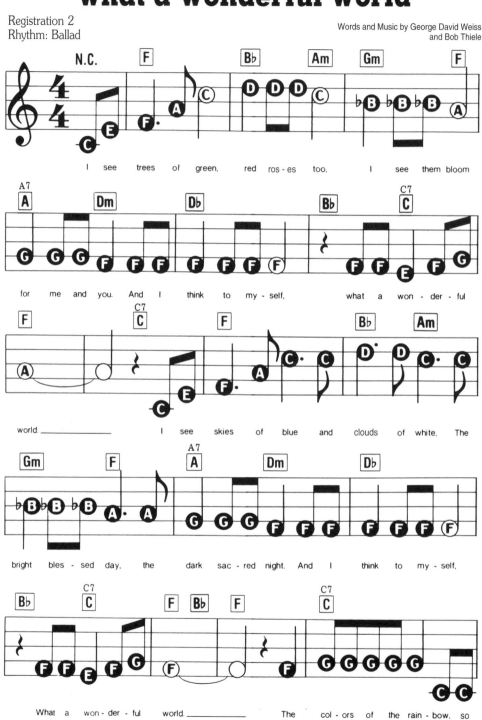

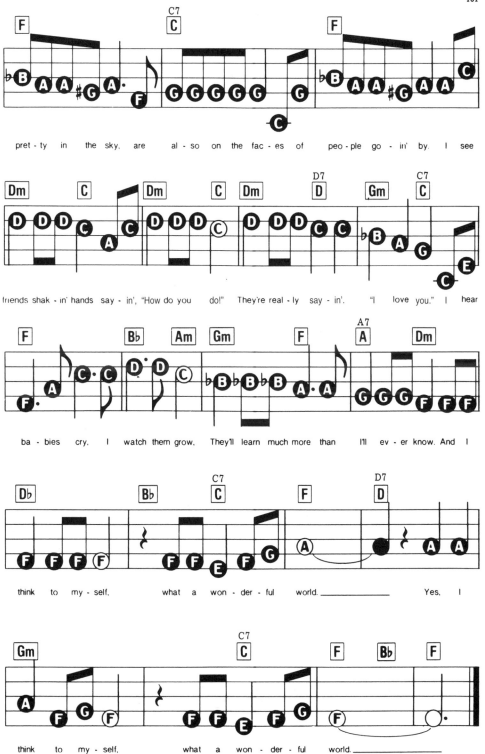

What Is This Thing Called Love?

from WAKE UP AND DREAM

Registration 7
Rhythm: Fox Trot or Swing

Words and Music by
Cole Porter

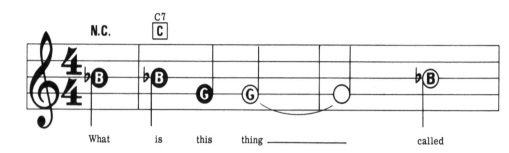

What is this thing _____ called

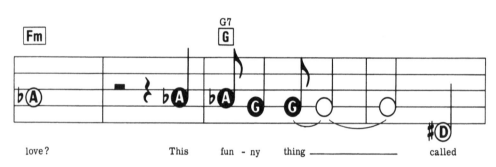

love? This fun - ny thing _____ called

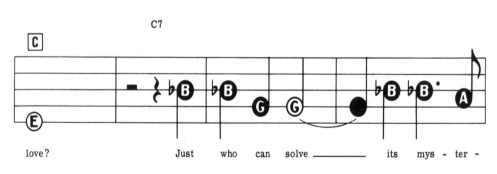

love? Just who can solve _____ its mys - ter -

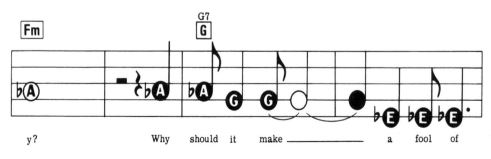

y? Why should it make _____ a fool of

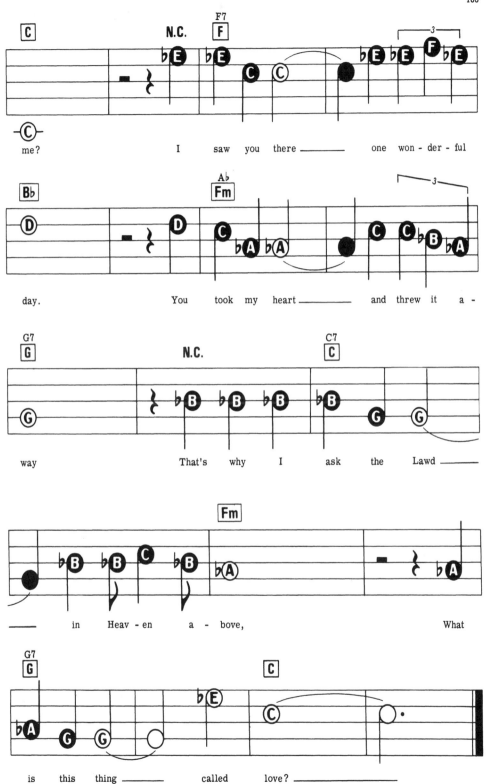

me? I saw you there ———— one won-der-ful

day. You took my heart ———— and threw it a-

way That's why I ask the Lawd ————

———— in Heav-en a - bove, What

is this thing ———— called love? ————

When I Fall in Love
from ONE MINUTE TO ZERO

Registration 10
Rhythm: Ballad or Fox Trot

Words by Edward Heyman
Music by Victor Young

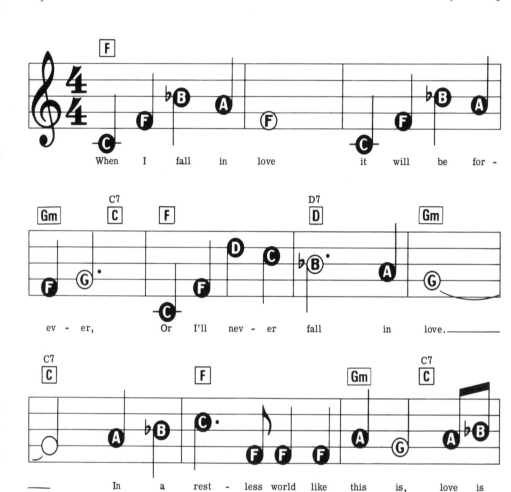

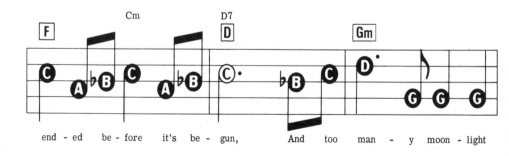

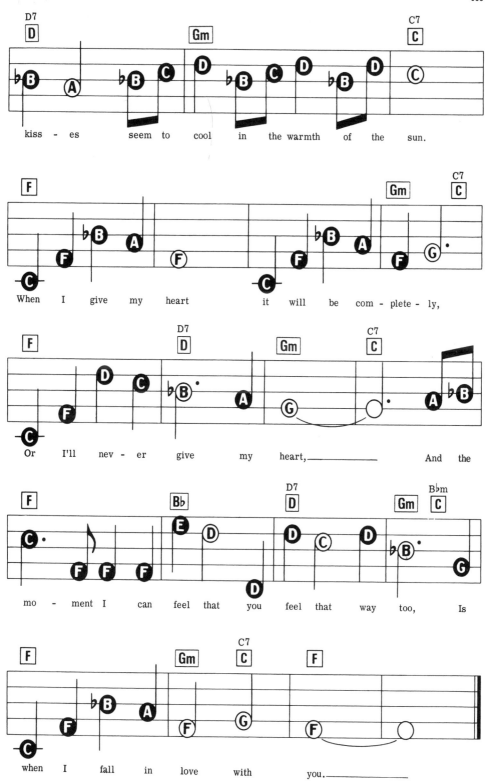

When You Wish Upon a Star

Registration 1
Rhythm: Ballad

Words by Ned Washington
Music by Leigh Harline

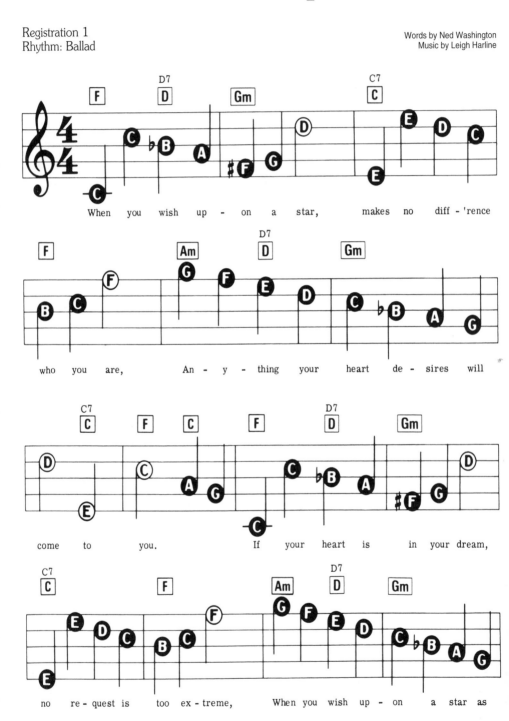

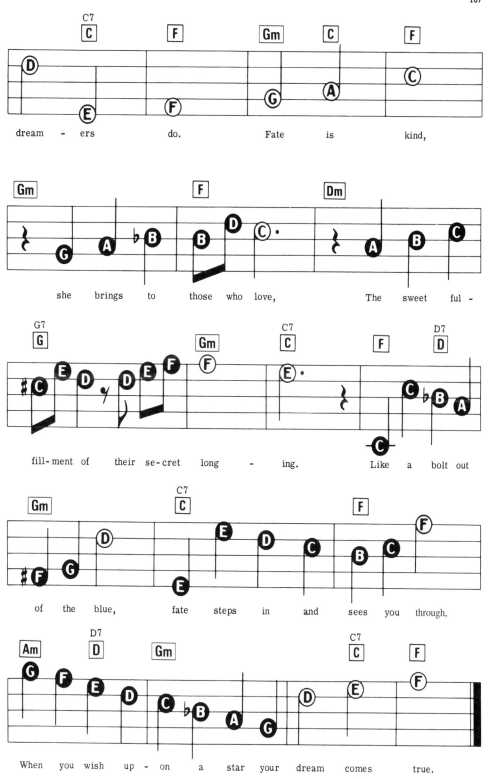

Yesterday

Registration 2
Rhythm: Rock or Ballad

Words and Music by John Lennon
and Paul McCartney

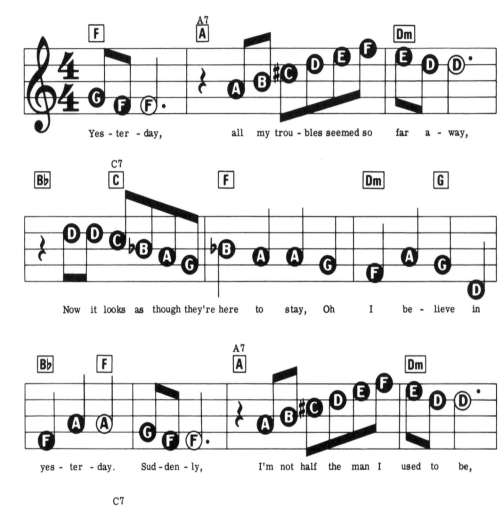

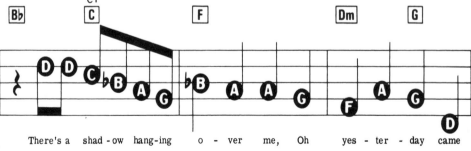

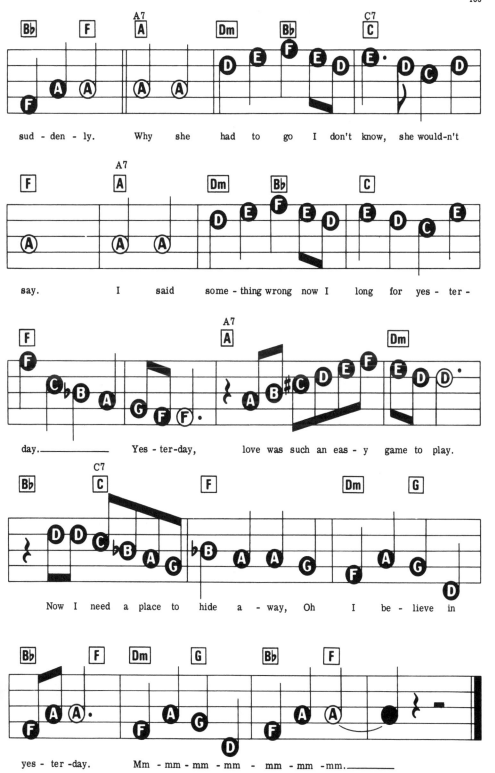

You Are So Beautiful

Registration 1
Rhythm: Pops or 8-Beat

Words and Music by Billy Preston
and Bruce Fisher

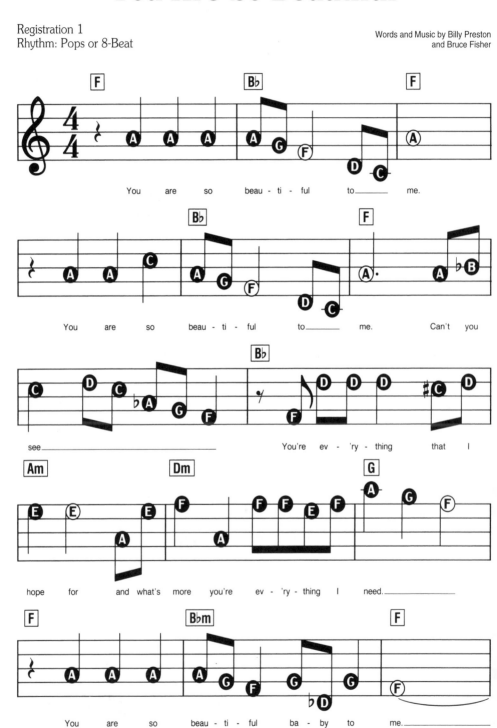

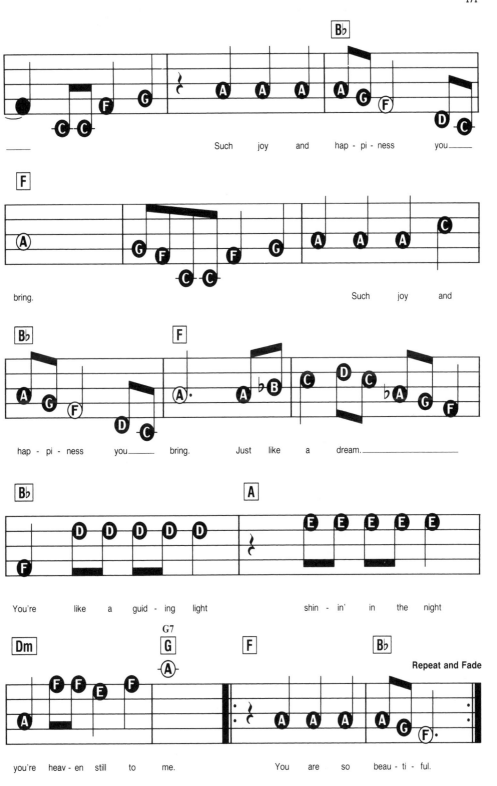

You Are the Sunshine of My Life

Registration 7
Rhythm: 8-Beat or Bossa Nova

Words and Music by
Stevie Wonder

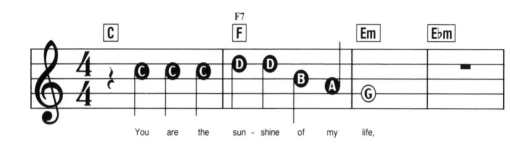

You are the sun - shine of my life,

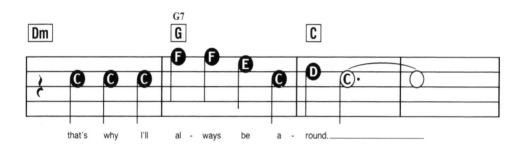

that's why I'll al - ways be a - round.

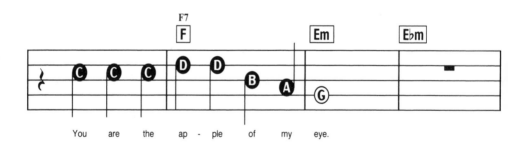

You are the ap - ple of my eye.

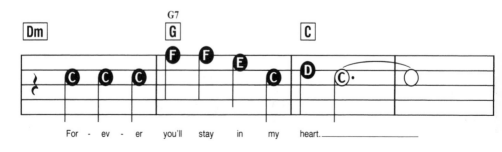

For - ev - er you'll stay in my heart.

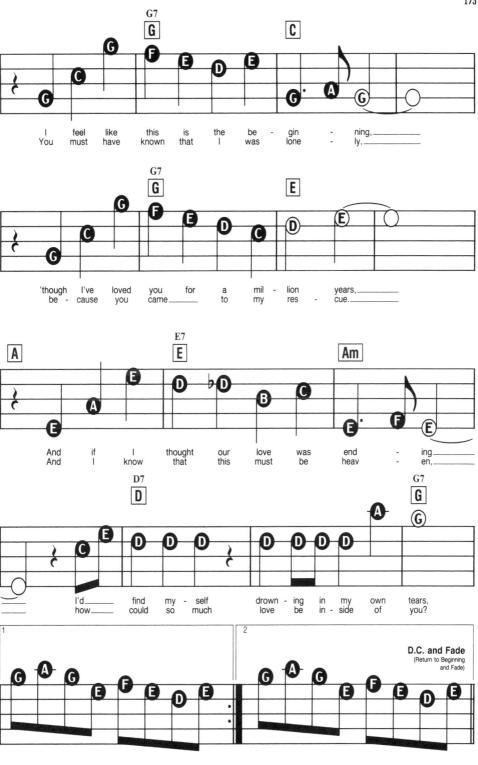

You Raise Me Up

Registration 3
Rhythm: Ballad

Words and Music by Brendan Graham
and Rolf Lovland

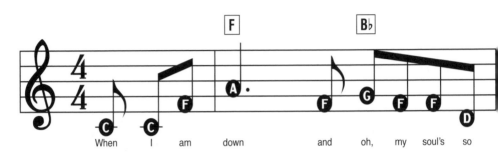

When   I   am   down   and   oh,   my   soul's   so

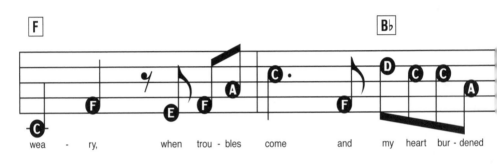

wea - ry,   when   trou - bles   come   and   my   heart   bur - dened

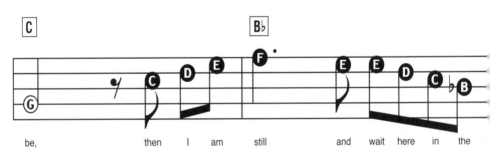

be,   then   I   am   still   and   wait   here   in   the

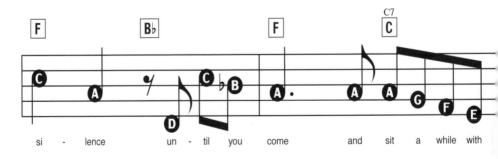

si - lence   un - til   you   come   and   sit   a   while   with

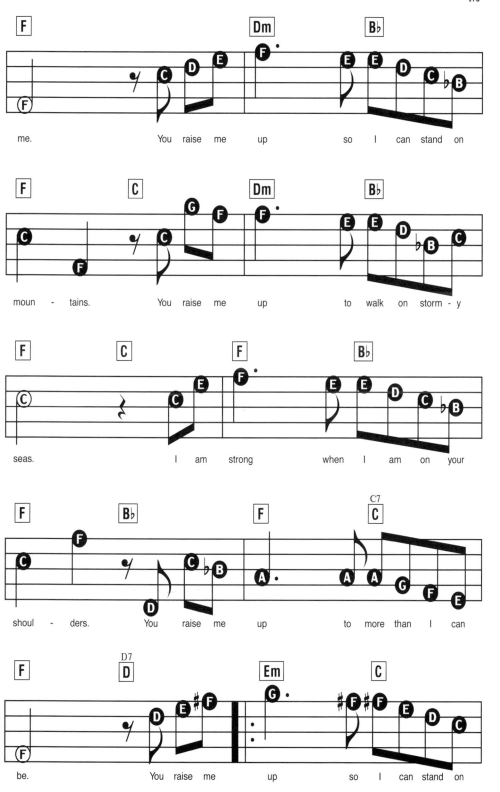

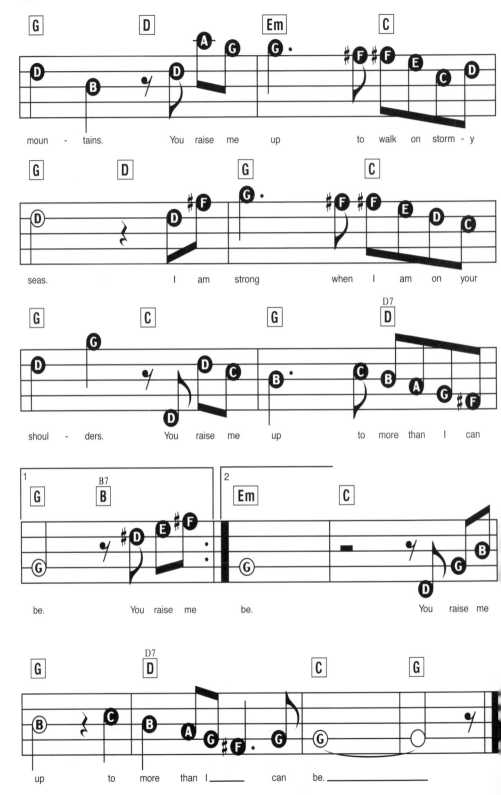